Digital Marketing Content Creation

Engaging Your Target Audience

JOHN LEWIS

DISCLAIMER

The contents of the book "**Digital Marketing Content Creation**," including, but not limited to, the text, graphics, images, and other material contained within, are the exclusive property of the author and are protected under international copyright laws.

TABLE OF CONTENTS

INTRODUCTION

Digital marketing is a larger term that encompasses e-marketing principles. Digital marketing tactics include digital media such as the Internet, social media, email, digital billboards, mobile applications, virtual reality, and databases. Audio, video, text, and images are all examples of digital media material. Digital marketing analytics is critical to the effectiveness of digital marketing campaigns, particularly when Big Data, Machine Learning, and Deep Learning models are used to anticipate user behaviors, purchasing patterns, and customer loyalty and retention.

As of April 2023, there were 5.18 billion internet users worldwide, which amounted to 64.6% of the global population. Of this total, 4.8 billion, or 59.9% of the world's population, were social media users. That implies that no matter what industry you're in, you'll most likely be able to contact your target audience online. You can take your time and gradually incorporate digital marketing methods and social media platforms, or you can dive right in and make digital marketing your top focus.

You need a clear path that will keep you from wasting time on things that don't matter. The most attractive website is a nice goal. Still, you will only be successful if you accomplish important things like developing amazing content, properly targeting your audience, and collecting important data.

People spend time online for various reasons, such as social media networking and Internet searching. The Internet has altered how customers perceive and share information about a product or service. It also allows consumers to make purchasing decisions more quickly than before. As a result, organizations must have dynamic strategies in place to understand the demands of their users and turn them into potential consumers.

Understanding the Role of Content in Digital Marketing

In digital marketing, content serves as the lifeblood that fuels interactions between businesses and their audience. It is the conduit through which ideas, emotions, and messages are conveyed, allowing brands to convey their unique identity, value propositions, and solutions to the challenges faced by their customers. Whether it's an insightful blog post, an eye-catching infographic, an entertaining social media video, or a comprehensive ebook, the diverse forms of content serve a common purpose – engaging, educating, and entertaining.

Content transcends the traditional boundaries of advertising by focusing on providing value rather than simply promoting products or services. By addressing the pain points and aspirations of the audience, content fosters genuine connections, establishes authority, and builds trust over time. The digital landscape offers myriad channels – from websites and social media platforms to podcasts and webinars – through which content can be distributed, allowing businesses to reach their target demographic with precision and relevance.

However, the art of digital marketing content creation isn't just about churning out pieces of information; it's about crafting a seamless and consistent narrative that aligns with the brand's values, resonates with the audience's interests, and adapts to ever-evolving trends and preferences. By harnessing the power of data analytics, businesses can gain insights into what works and what doesn't, enabling them to refine their content strategies for maximum impact.

The Power of Compelling Content: Building Relationships and Driving Conversions

Compelling content can captivate and engage audiences, driving them to act and increasing conversions. Let's explore the concept of compelling content, its significance in delivering quality content, and how it effectively drives engagement and conversions.

Every marketing strategy deserves quality content that forms the foundation for driving engagement and conversion to their content. Quality content is key to building trust, establishing authority, and nurturing relationships with your audience.

According to the Content Marketing Institute, 73% of B2B and 70% of B2C marketers use content marketing as part of their overall marketing strategy. Hence, even the most enticing marketing campaigns may fall flat without quality content.

When content is engaging, it captivates users' attention, encourages them to interact, and motivates them to take desired actions. Let's see how compelling content drives engagement;

Captivating Attention: Compelling content must capture the reader's or viewer's attention. It uses strong headlines, captivating visuals, and engaging storytelling techniques to connect immediately and keep the audience engaged. 48% of marketers said original graphics (infographics, illustrations) helped them reach their marketing goals in 2023.

Creating Emotional Connections: Tapping into the emotional aspect of human nature establishes a deeper connection with your audience, making them more likely to engage with the content and share it with others. Compelling content can evoke strong emotions such as joy, surprise, inspiration, or even empathy. It is said that if your content does not connect with your target audience, then your reach will be poor. The people viewing your content are humans with emotions, so creating content that resonates with them is important.

Encouraging Interaction: Engagement is king when it comes to content. Compelling content encourages audience interaction through comments, likes, shares, and discussions. Although some thought leaders would say that likes and shares amount to conversion. I rather differ in my opinion; an interaction that sparks more conversations invites opinions and fosters a sense of community around the content, leading to increased engagement and brand loyalty.

Providing Value: Content marketing is equivalent to value delivery, and creating compelling content is building a value system for which you will certainly be rewarded. Compelling content provides genuine value to the audience. It educates, informs, entertains, or solves a problem for the readers or viewers. When people find value in the content, they are more likely to engage with it, share it, and seek more content from the same source.

How Compelling Content Drives Conversions

Content marketing generates three times as many leads as traditional outbound marketing but costs 62% less.

Building Trust and Credibility: Consistently delivering high-quality, valuable content establishes you as an authority in your industry. Compelling content creates trust and credibility for your brand or business. Businesses thrive on the foundation of trust and credibility, but lacking it is losing customers. This trust and credibility make the audience more receptive to your offerings and more likely to convert into customers.

Showcasing Expertise: Compelling content allows you to showcase your expertise and demonstrate your knowledge and understanding of your target audience's pain points and challenges. By providing solutions and insights, you position yourself as a reliable source of information and a trusted advisor, which increases the chances of conversion. Expertise is proof of quality. 83% of marketers believe it's more effective to create higher quality content less often.

Call-to-Action (CTA) Integration: In the customer journey, there is no conversion without a CTA; copywriting gurus will always say people love being told what to do. Compelling content strategically incorporates clear and persuasive calls to action. Whether it's directing the audience to sign up for a newsletter, download an ebook, or make a purchase, a well-crafted CTA within compelling content can significantly increase conversion rates.

Amplifying Reach: Compelling content is more likely to be shared and recommended by your audience. 92% of consumers trust referrals from people they know – Nielsen. This organic sharing extends your reach to a wider audience, increasing the chances of reaching potential customers who may convert based on the compelling content they encounter.

Conclusively, investing time and resources in crafting high-quality, unique, and valuable content that resonates with your target audience is crucial to harness the true power of compelling content. Compelling content serves as a powerful tool in driving engagement and conversions. To engage your audience, capture attention, create emotional connections, and provide value. People are more likely to remember and respond to interesting, meaningful, and helpful information.

UNDERSTANDING YOUR AUDIENCE

In the dynamic landscape of digital marketing, one of the foundational pillars of creating effective and engaging content is a deep understanding of your target audience. This understanding goes beyond superficial demographics and delves into the intricate web of interests, aspirations, and challenges that shape the behaviors and decisions of your potential customers. Crafting content that resonates requires a comprehensive grasp of your audience, what they care about, and how your brand can provide value to them.

Customers' attention is drawn to what they have to say and sell. The fight for attention has been severe since introducing the "always on" culture. In truth, half of the content businesses produce is never seen by their prospects. It wasn't always difficult to catch people's attention. When you wanted to catch a customer's attention in the past century, you would send him marketing material and call him. The prospect was usually receptive because you were the curator of all product knowledge. Those days, however, are long gone.

Conversely, conversations assist in building relationships, and relationships help you get and maintain your customer's attention. So, how can you compete for consumers' attention with other producers? There is no scarcity of content from your rivals, identifying each of them as the best option. Your content is most likely doing the same thing. You may or may not be able to see your customers in person, but you must engage them with great content that solves their requirements and gives relevant information.

Defining Your Target Audience: Demographics, Interests, and Pain Points

One of the foundational pillars for crafting effective content is a deep understanding of your target audience. Gone are the days of one-size-fits-all approaches; today's digital landscape demands a tailored and personalized approach that resonates with specific groups of individuals. Delving into your audience's demographics, interests, and pain points is crucial to accomplish this.

Demographics: Demographics provide the foundational framework for understanding your audience's basic characteristics. This includes factors such as age, gender, location, marital status, income level, education, and occupation. These statistics offer valuable insights into the background of your audience, allowing you to create content that speaks directly to their life stages, aspirations, and challenges.

Interests: Delving into the interests and preferences of your target audience goes beyond surface-level demographics. It involves understanding what they are passionate about, their hobbies, and what kind of content resonates with them. Analyze their online behaviors – the websites they visit, the social media platforms they engage with, and the types of content they consume. This knowledge enables you to craft content that aligns with their passions, making it more likely to capture and retain their attention.

Pain Points: To truly connect with your audience, you must address their pain points – the challenges, frustrations, and problems they encounter. Identifying these pain points requires empathy and research. Engage in conversations with your existing customers, conduct surveys, analyze customer support inquiries, and monitor social media discussions. By pinpointing the issues your audience is grappling with, you can tailor your content to provide solutions and insights that resonate deeply.

Creating a Persona: Combining these insights, creating a buyer persona is beneficial – a semi-fictional representation of your ideal customer. This persona encapsulates your target audience's demographics, interests, and pain points in a relatable and humanized form. Giving this persona a name, a backstory, and even a photo can help you and your team better visualize and empathize with your audience, leading to more strategic content creation.

Concentrating on Attention

Unsurprisingly, technology has reduced attention span. According to the Statistic Brain Institute, attention span is "the amount of concentrated time on a task without becoming distracted" and was 12 seconds in 2000 but has now dropped to 8.25 seconds. According to the Statistic Brain Institute, an office worker checks her email roughly thirty times every hour. When multiplied by an 8-hour day, that's a startling statistic. Every day, two hundred and forty times!

Looking for the "Attention Web"

So, why does the average customer's attention span and distractibility matter to you as a digital marketer? It matters since you want to get your prospect's attention, which is becoming increasingly tough daily. Furthermore, what marketers have come to assume about engagement metrics (that they consist of metrics such as page views or clicks) may be incorrect. As a result, marketers began to examine whether consumers' time engaging with content or scrolling would be better indicators of their interest. This sparked the "attention web" movement, which involves selling ads based on attention metrics rather than mere numbers (for example, clicks).

Using the click as the primary attention metric was determined to be incorrect. Two known myths provided are as follows:

- **Myth: We only read what we click on.**

  This appears to be a common-sense assumption, yet it may not be. You expect that the reader will read the article after clicking on it. This may be true, but it does not necessarily imply that the reader takes the time to read the article.

  They might glance at it and then go on. The content marketer is ecstatic about the number of hits they receive, but the reader may not relate to the brand. The content marketer publishes more similar content with the false notion that his reader is engaged. You can see how this might have a detrimental influence on your entire content strategy.

- **Myth: We read more if we share more.**

  You'd think that a person would only share articles that he considered interesting. This is yet another misconception. People share for various reasons. Haile discovered no association between the amount of time spent on an article and the number of shares, shattering the notion that such pieces have achieved their goal. People may distribute stories based on their headlines and sources. Based on these characteristics, they guess how relevant the content is to their audience.

According to research, the following should be used:

- **Mini-graphics**: These graphics focus on a single data rather than an entire infographic. This strategy is valuable since it employs a picture to catch attention while not requiring the reader to spend too much time figuring it out.

- **Brief lists**: A brief list appeals to those who are always on the go. You deliver knowledge in bite-sized portions, much like a snack.

- **How-to articles**: Once again, you can see how this format can be tailored to a reader with a short attention span. You can focus on learning how to accomplish one item, as you did with the mini-graphic.

- **Tips & tricks**: This approach is popular with all audiences. You captivate attention without slowing down the reader by reducing the content to a few pieces.

- **FAQs (frequently asked questions)**: Keep them brief and answer only one question each. In this manner, you aid readers' development rather than slowing them down with fluff.

- **Social media posts**: Some of these posts should be brief and to the point. If the reader is interested, don't pass up the opportunity to publish short content that links to a longer-form piece.

Aside from producing content designed for short attention spans, marketers and researchers have been looking for ways to improve their measurements to gauge genuine reader interest.

Examining Attention Triggers

Although some may regard attention as an unknowable commodity, there are prescribed methods for capturing it. Former Mashable editor Ben Parr discusses seven attention-grabbing triggers. These triggers are collected from the realms of psychology and neuroscience and will help you understand how and why individuals pay attention (sometimes without consciously thinking about it).

The catalysts include:

- **"Automaticity"**: This trigger is based on people's automatic responses to sensory stimuli such as color.

- **Framing**: This trigger draws individuals in by challenging their worldview. This indicates that when you deliver anything in an unexpected or non-intuitive way, you capture people's attention. You have presented the issue in a way that does not correspond to their comprehension.

- **Disruption**: Using the disruption trigger upsets a person's expectations, causing them to pay attention.

- **Reward**: Using the reward trigger, you may tap into people's natural desire for rewards.

- **Reputation**: This trigger is based on the notion that people believe experts' words and will pay attention to them.

- **Mystery**: When individuals are unsure what will happen or don't comprehend something, they pay attention until they find out.

- **Acknowledgment**: People readily acknowledge those who nurture and support them.

Looking over this list, you may conclude that attracting attention is less mysterious than you previously believed. The issue with developing content is that you must know your audience well enough to know what constitutes a trigger.

Buyer Personas: Creating Detailed Profiles to Guide Your Content Strategy

Creating effective and engaging content in digital marketing isn't a shot in the dark; it's a strategic process that hinges on a deep understanding of your target audience. One of the most powerful tools for achieving this understanding is the concept of buyer personas. Buyer personas are detailed, semi-fictional representations of your ideal customers crafted through research, data analysis, and empathy. These personas go beyond surface-level demographics and provide a comprehensive insight into the motivations, behaviors, pain points, and aspirations that drive your audience's decisions.

Crafting Comprehensive Buyer Personas

- **Research and Data Collection:** Start by collecting data from various sources, such as customer surveys, website analytics, social media insights, and customer feedback. This data should cover demographics, psychographics, online behaviors, and preferences.

- **Identify Commonalities:** Analyze the collected data to identify patterns and common traits among your audience. Look for shared interests, challenges, goals, and buying behaviors that can help you group your audience into distinct personas.

- **Empathy and Understanding:** To truly connect with your audience, you need to step into their shoes. Imagine their daily lives, their pain points, and the solutions they seek. What motivates them to make decisions? What obstacles do they encounter?

- **Detailed Persona Profiles:** Once you've collected and analyzed the data, create detailed persona profiles. Give each persona a name, a backstory, and a set of characteristics. Include information about their age, job role, goals, hobbies, preferred social platforms, challenges, and objections to purchasing.

- **Segmentation:** Depending on your business and audience diversity, you may have multiple buyer personas. Segment your personas based on factors like industry, buying intent, or engagement level. This segmentation will help tailor your content even further.

Guiding Your Content Strategy with Buyer Personas

- **Content Relevance:** Armed with detailed personas, your content can be crafted to resonate directly with each persona's interests, challenges, and aspirations. This relevance increases the likelihood of engagement and conversion.

- **Tone and Style:** Each persona might respond differently to tones and styles of communication. A professional might prefer formal language, while a person interested in creative fields might appreciate a casual approach.

- **Content Format:** Different personas may prefer different content formats – from blog posts and videos to infographics and podcasts. Tailor your content formats to match the preferences of each persona.

- **Addressing Pain Points:** Create content that addresses each persona's pain points and challenges. This positions your brand as a solution provider and establishes credibility and trust.

- **Nurturing Journeys:** Map out the buyer's journey for each persona, from awareness to consideration and decision-making. Craft content that guides them through each stage, offering the information they need at every step.

- **Personalized Marketing:** Utilize your personas to personalize email marketing, social media campaigns, and other communication efforts. Personalization enhances engagement and fosters a sense of connection.

- **Feedback Loop:** Continuously gather feedback and data on how your content resonates with each persona. Adjust your content strategy based on these insights to ensure ongoing relevance.

Creating detailed buyer personas empowers your digital marketing content strategy by humanizing your audience. It allows you to go beyond viewing your audience as faceless numbers and instead understand the unique individuals interacting with your brand. By aligning your content strategy with the needs and preferences of your personas, you'll be better equipped to forge meaningful connections, drive engagement, and guide your audience toward conversion and brand loyalty.

Conducting Audience Research: Surveys, Analytics, and Social Listening

In digital marketing, understanding your audience is paramount to crafting content that resonates and engages. Conducting thorough audience research equips you with the insights needed to tailor your content strategy to meet your target demographic's preferences, needs, and behaviors. You can employ several powerful methods to gather valuable information about your audience: surveys, analytics, and social listening.

Surveys: Unveiling Insights Directly from Your Audience

Surveys are a direct and effective way to collect specific information from your audience. By designing well-structured surveys, you can ask targeted questions to uncover preferences, pain points, and motivations. Online survey tools make it easy to create and distribute surveys through various channels, such as email, social media, and your website.

Tips for Effective Surveys

- Keep surveys concise and focused to maintain participant engagement.
- Use a mix of open-ended and multiple-choice questions to gather both quantitative and qualitative data.
- Include questions about demographics, interests, and challenges to build well-rounded audience profiles.
- Incentivize participation with rewards or exclusive content to encourage higher response rates.

Analytics: Extracting Insights from Digital Footprints

Website and social media analytics offer a treasure trove of data about your audience's behaviors and interactions. Tools like Google Analytics provide information about website traffic, user demographics, page views, and conversion rates. Social media insights offer similar data, revealing engagement metrics, follower demographics, and popular content.

Tips for Effective Analytics Usage

- Analyze user behavior patterns to understand which content resonates the most.
- Identify traffic sources to determine where your audience is finding your content.
- Examine bounce rates to gauge how engaging your content is and where improvements are needed.
- Use conversion tracking to measure the effectiveness of your content in driving desired actions.

Social Listening: Tapping into Conversations and Sentiments

Social listening involves monitoring online conversations and discussing your brand, industry, or niche. Using social media listening tools, you can track mentions, hashtags, and keywords to gain insights into what people say about your brand and topics relevant to your audience.

Tips for Effective Social Listening

- Monitor conversations across various social media platforms to gather a holistic view of sentiment and trends.
- Pay attention to positive and negative feedback to understand what resonates and needs improvement.
- Identify emerging topics and trends that can inform your content strategy.
- Engage in relevant conversations to build relationships and demonstrate your brand's expertise.

You can comprehensively understand your audience's preferences, behaviors, and needs by leveraging surveys, analytics, and social listening. This informed approach allows you to create content that speaks directly to your audience, enhancing engagement and building stronger relationships. Audience research is not a one-time endeavor but an ongoing process, ensuring your content remains relevant and impactful as your audience evolves.

SETTING CONTENT GOALS AND STRATEGY

A content strategy is the process of planning, creating, publishing, managing, and governing content. A smart content strategy will attract and engage a target audience while addressing their demands and advancing business objectives.

Assume one of your company's objectives is to raise brand recognition. You may execute an SEO-focused content strategy to boost your website's exposure on search engine results pages (SERPs) and generate visitors to your products or services.

Early on, new business owners may believe a content strategy is a nice-to-have but not critical. However, creating high-quality content can be invaluable in terms of establishing trust with new audiences and long-term success. A smart content strategy is the cornerstone of the Attract and Delight stages of an inbound marketing buyer's journey. A content strategy can be used for sales enablement, customer happiness, and enticing prospects for your business.

Furthermore, with 70% of marketers actively spending on content marketing, developing a robust content strategy is vital to competing in your business.

Content marketing helps firms prepare for consistent and cost-effective website traffic sources and new leads. If you can write just one blog post that receives consistent organic traffic, an embedded link to an ebook or free tool will continue to generate leads for you long after you press "Publish."

The consistent flow of visitors and leads generated by your evergreen content will allow you to experiment with various revenue-generating marketing methods, such as sponsored content, social media advertising, and distributed content. Furthermore, your material will help attract leads, educate your prospects, and raise brand awareness.

Setting Content Goals and Strategy: Defining Clear Objectives

In the dynamic digital marketing landscape, a well-defined content strategy is essential to guide your efforts toward achieving specific objectives. Clear objectives provide direction, focus, and measurable outcomes that help you assess the success of your content initiatives. When setting content goals, consider key objectives such as brand awareness, lead generation, conversion, and more.

Brand Awareness

Objective: To increase your brand's visibility and recognition among your target audience.

Strategy:

- Create informative and engaging content that educates your audience about your industry, products, or services.
- Leverage social media platforms to share your content and engage with your audience.
- Collaborate with influencers or other industry experts to amplify your reach.
- Focus on shareable and visually appealing content to maximize exposure.

Lead Generation

Objective: To attract and capture potential customers, nurturing them through the sales funnel.

Strategy:

- Develop high-value content such as ebooks, whitepapers, or webinars that require users to provide their contact information in exchange for access.
- Implement strong calls-to-action (CTAs) that guide visitors to relevant landing pages.
- Personalize content to different stages of the buyer's journey, addressing their pain points and interests.
- Use lead magnets, like free trials or exclusive offers, to entice users to engage further.

Conversion

Objective: To encourage users to take a specific action that contributes directly to your business goals, such as making a purchase or signing up for a service.

Strategy:

- Craft persuasive and compelling content that emphasizes the value of your products or services.
- Create landing pages optimized for conversions, featuring clear, concise information and a strong CTA.
- To build trust and credibility, incorporate social proof elements, such as testimonials and case studies.
- Implement retargeting strategies to reach users who have previously engaged with your content.

Engagement and Relationship Building:

Objective: To foster a deeper connection with your audience, encouraging repeat visits and building brand loyalty.

Strategy:

- Develop interactive content like quizzes, polls, and contests to engage users actively.
- Respond to comments and messages on social media platforms to encourage dialogue.
- Share user-generated content and stories to showcase your community.
- Implement email marketing campaigns to nurture relationships and keep your audience informed.

Thought Leadership and Authority

Objective: To position your brand as an industry leader and a reliable source of information.

Strategy:

- Create in-depth, well-researched content that provides valuable insights into your industry.
- Publish blog posts, articles, and reports that address emerging trends and challenges.
- Participate in webinars, podcasts, or conferences to share your expertise.
- Collaborate with other experts or thought leaders to enhance your credibility.

Customer Education

Objective: To educate your audience about your products or services, helping them make informed decisions.

Strategy:

- Develop tutorials, how-to guides, and instructional videos to showcase your offerings.
- Address common customer questions and concerns through informative content.
- Use case studies to demonstrate how your products or services have solved real-world problems.
- Provide clear comparisons between your offerings and competitors to help users make educated choices.

Remember that setting SMART goals (Specific, Measurable, Achievable, Relevant, and Time-bound) is essential for effective content strategy execution. Tailor your content approach to your chosen objectives, continuously monitor performance, and refine your strategy based on data-driven insights to maximize the impact of your content efforts.

Mapping Content to the Customer Journey: Awareness, Consideration, Decision

If your company has even one customer, you already have a customer journey in place. This customer path may not have been developed intentionally, but it does exist. In your organization, perhaps you refer to it as a "marketing (or sales) pipeline."

Whatever you call it, the goal of your marketing is to become intentional about moving cold prospects, leads, and existing customers through the stages of this journey. When you effectively map out your ideal customer journey, you immediately identify the bottlenecks preventing the flow of prospects to leads, leads to customers, and customers to enthusiastic fans.

The importance of sequence in marketing, particularly in digital marketing, cannot be overstated. Cold prospects must be moved from one stage of the customer journey to the next seamlessly and subtly. You're not going to turn a stranger into a brand enthusiast overnight. However, you can gradually transfer the prospect from one level of the relationship to the next. Follow the eight steps below to guide individuals through the customer journey stages.

8 Steps Through the Customer Journey

Step 1: Raise Awareness

Every repeat consumer and enthusiastic lover of your brand was once a total stranger to your organization. She had no notion of what problem you were solving, what products you were selling, or what your brand represented. The first step on her path from cold prospect to screaming fan is becoming aware. We go into more detail regarding techniques later in this book, but if you want to raise awareness, use the following digital marketing tactics:

- **Advertising:** Both online and offline advertising is a reliable and effective technique for creating awareness.

- **Social Media Marketing:** Every day, billions of people use social media sites such as Facebook, Twitter, and LinkedIn. Social media marketing is a low-cost way to raise awareness.

- **Search Marketing:** Every day, billions of web queries are processed on sites such as Google and Bing. Some of the traffic is directed to your website by simple search marketing strategies.

Step 2: Increasing Engagement

Making a cold prospect aware of your company, products, and brand isn't enough. You must design your marketing to capture and engage your prospect's attention. Engagement for a digital marketer usually takes the form of valuable material provided freely available in the form of blog entries.

- Podcasts
- Online Videos

A prospect, lead, or customer may spend a few minutes to several years in any of the customer journey stages. A prospect, for example, may become aware of your blog and engage with it for a year or more before going on to the next stage of the journey. Others will rush through various journey stages in a matter of minutes. A healthy company has people at all phases of the journey at all times.

Step 3: Gathering Subscribers

The next phase in the customer journey is to move a prospect from the "merely aware and engaged" stage to the subscriber or lead stage.

A subscriber is somebody who has permitted you to speak with him. Subscriber lists are built by savvy digital marketers using social media connections on sites like Facebook and Twitter, garnering podcast subscribers on services like iTunes and Stitcher, or creating subscribers through webinar registrations.

Offline businesses may create online subscriptions by allowing active prospects to get physical mail or request a consultative sales call or product demo. However, email subscription is the Holy Grail of lead generation in the digital marketing world. Email is by far the cheapest and most effective way of moving a prospect through the remaining stages of the customer journey.

Step 4: Boosting Conversions

This step aims to increase the prospect's commitment level by asking for a small amount of time or money. Low-cost items or services, webinars, and product demonstrations are all excellent offers to provide at this time.

The relationship with this prospect has remained passive throughout the first three stages of the customer journey. The goal of Stage 4 is not revenue but a stronger bond between the prospect and your company. GoDaddy is one company that provides this greater connectivity by, among other things, allowing you to register a domain name for a website and host and create one for your business.

Step 5: Create Excitement

Your marketing should purposefully push your customers to take advantage of the deal they accepted in Step 4. Customer onboarding is the commercial phrase for getting your prospect to take advantage of an offer. Whether the conversion in Step 4 was a financial or time commitment, the relationship with this client or prospect is far more likely to succeed if she gained value from the transaction.

The worth of your offers should transcend the price paid by your customer. Deliver excellent products and services while developing marketing efforts to promote their use. After all, if your consumers aren't using the product or service, they're unlikely to buy it again or recommend it to others.

Step 6: Sell the Main Offer and More

Prospects have formed a bond with your brand at this point. They may have spent some time or money on you. People who form this bond with your organization are far more likely to purchase a more sophisticated, costly, or risky product or service from you. This transition from passive prospect to buyer is referred to as ascension.

Unfortunately, this is where most firms' marketing begins and ends. Some chilly prospects are asked to make dangerous investments of time and money with a company they know nothing about. This is the equivalent of proposing marriage on a first date: the chances of success are slim. Other brands quit marketing to a customer once that client has converted (purchased) rather than remaining in touch with that person and converting that person into a repeat shopper.

Customers or prospects in the ascension stage buy high-ticket items or services, sign up for subscriptions that bill them monthly, or become devoted, repeat buyers. Assuming you've put in the effort in Stages 1-5 of the customer journey, you should find that some of your leads and customers are eager to buy more and buy again. This is because you've established a rapport with them and effectively articulated the value you can provide to their life. When you appeal to your clients in this order, they will likely become brand supporters and promoters.

Step 7: Recruiting Brand Ambassadors

Brand advocates provide testimonials about their fantastic experience with your brand. They are supporters of your company and defend it on social media networks. They will submit positive reviews for your products or services on sites like Yelp or Amazon if requested.

Your relationship with these leads and buyers determines your potential to develop brand supporters. When you get to this point, your consumer and your firm are like close friends in the sense that getting to this point took time and effort, and maintaining that relationship — one that is mutually advantageous to both parties — will likewise take time and work.

You establish this relationship by offering value, delivering on your product's promise (that it truly performs what you say it will do), and providing timely customer support. You may turn consumers into brand advocates and promoters by constantly giving exceptional products and services.

Step 8: Recruiting Brand Advocates

Company promoters go over and above advocacy, tattooing your emblem across their chest (think Harley Davidson), devoting hours of their leisure time to blogging and using social media to communicate their love of your company online. The difference between a brand promoter and an advocate (Step 7) is that the promoter actively spreads the word about your company, while the advocate is more passive.

Your company has become a part of the lives of brand promoters. They see your brand as one on which they can rely. Brand promoters believe in you because your brand and goods consistently provide excellent value. They have given you not only their money but also their time.

Making a Customer Journey Road Map

The client journey does not happen by chance for successful organizations. Marketing campaigns designed by smart digital marketers purposefully drive prospects, leads, and consumers from one stage to the next. When you understand your ideal customer journey, the strategies that should be used (explained in the next chapters of this book) become evident.

Developing a customer journey road map that clearly defines the eight stages discussed in the last section of this chapter is an excellent method to plan and visualize the path that an ideal customer will follow from cold prospect to brand promoter. Gather your company's stakeholders and create a customer journey map for at least one of your primary goods or services.

Consider which promotions and offers to utilize at each stage of the customer journey to raise awareness of your product and bring them from awareness to your ideal state of being a brand promoter.

Enhancing the Customer Journey

It's great that you documented your customer journey, but just because you did doesn't imply you're finished. When you've figured out and developed the customer experience for your company, it's time to optimize it. The client journey is not something that can be laminated once completed.

It's not something you can leave alone. If you want your business to thrive, you'll need to reassess and fine-tune your customer journey as your company and customers evolve.

You should review and optimize your customer journey every time you add, remove or update a product or service. If you introduce a new customer persona to your firm, it's time to optimize your customer journey again.

Avoiding an Optimization Error

When you first start optimizing your customer journey, your instinct may be to start at the beginning, with Step 1: raising awareness. But it isn't where you want to begin. In fact, when optimizing your customer journey, the awareness stage is the last place you want to start.

Why?

As the phrase goes, starting from the beginning is like pouring more water into a leaky bucket. All of your efforts to optimize the first phases of the customer journey will be futile if you have gaps later in the trip that cause your clients to become stuck or not convert at all.

To avoid this issue, you should not concentrate your optimization efforts at the start of the journey. Instead, you'll begin near the end of your adventure.

It is best to begin optimizing your client journey at the ascent stage (Step 6). Begin with the question, "How can I increase the average customer value?" "How do I get rid of the bottlenecks that are keeping the customer stuck?" You can maximize your earnings by filling any gaps in the ascension stage. And with greater profit, you'll be able to put more money into your business path (rather than dumping leads and consumers into a leaking bucket).

Work backward when you've maximized the ascension stage.

- Optimize your excitement stage (Step 5).
- Then, optimize your convert stage (Step 4).
- Then, the subscribe stage (Step 3).
- Followed by the engage stage (Step 2).
- And finally, optimize the awareness stage (Step 1).

After optimizing the early stages of the customer journey, you focus on the latter two stages – brand advocates (Step 7) and brand promoters (Step 8), searching for ways to produce more of each.

Working on one stage at a time is critical to optimize your client experience. Concentrate all of your efforts on that one step before moving on to the next. Start a new stage only when you've fully optimized the one you're working on. In the same vein, don't work on numerous stages simultaneously. Resolve one stage at a time. If you bounce from step to stage or optimize numerous phases simultaneously, you'll likely miss holes and waste your time. Only optimizing one stage at a time allows you to seal all leaks and remove bottlenecks for your customers.

You're not just searching for holes to fill as you optimize each stage. You're looking for bottlenecks in the customer's journey, anything that keeps them stuck and prevents them from progressing to the next level. And you want to remove those impediments to fill those gaps and acquire more leads and customers at each stage of the customer journey.

Developing a Content Calendar: Balancing Frequency, Types, and Themes

A well-structured content calendar is the backbone of a successful digital marketing strategy. It ensures that your content efforts are organized, consistent, and aligned with your goals and audience preferences. When developing your content calendar, finding the right balance between content frequency, types, and themes is essential to keep your audience engaged and your brand's messaging on point.

Determine Content Frequency: Consider how often you can realistically create and publish quality content without sacrificing its quality. Your frequency might vary based on your resources, target audience, and the nature of your industry. Some businesses might post multiple times a day, while others might opt for a few high-quality pieces per week.

Vary Content Types: Mixing up content types keeps your audience engaged and caters to different preferences. Include a variety of formats, such as:

- **Blog Posts:** In-depth articles, how-to guides, listicles, and thought leadership pieces.

- **Videos:** Tutorials, interviews, product demos, and behind-the-scenes content.

- **Visuals:** Infographics, memes, and images that resonate with your brand and audience.

- **Podcasts:** Audio content on relevant topics, industry trends, and interviews.

- **Webinars:** Interactive sessions that offer valuable insights to your audience.

- **Social Media Posts:** Short and engaging content for platforms like Facebook, Instagram, Twitter, and LinkedIn.

Align with Themes: Creating content around consistent themes or topics helps establish your brand's expertise and gives your audience a reason to return. Themes can be related to your industry, seasonal trends, customer pain points, or current events. For example, a fitness brand might focus on themes like workout routines, nutrition tips, and mental well-being.

Maintain Consistency: A regular publishing schedule establishes a sense of consistency for your audience. Whether you post daily, weekly, or monthly, stick to your chosen schedule. This consistency builds trust and anticipation among your audience.

Plan Seasonal and Trending Content: Incorporate content related to holidays, special events, and trending topics. This shows your brand's relevance and adaptability to current conversations.

Include Evergreen Content: Alongside timely and trending content, including evergreen pieces that remain relevant over time. These resources continue to attract visitors and engagement long after their initial publication.

Distribute Content Across Channels: Adapt your content to various platforms and channels while maintaining a cohesive message. Each channel may have its own nuances, so tailor your content accordingly.

Monitor Analytics: Regularly review analytics to assess the performance of different content types, themes, and publishing frequencies. Use these insights to refine your content strategy over time.

Leave Room for Flexibility: While planning is crucial, leave some room for spontaneous content that addresses timely events or responds to audience interactions.

Collaboration and Delegation: If you have a team, delegate tasks and responsibilities to ensure that content creation, editing, and publishing processes run smoothly.

Developing a content calendar requires a balance between consistency and adaptability. By considering content frequency, types, and themes, you can create a holistic content strategy that engages your audience, supports your goals, and showcases your brand's unique voice and expertise.

CRAFTING COMPELLING CONTENT

It is quite evident how vital compelling content is by now, but how do you create outstanding content and then put it out there for your audience? To be effective, you must first recognize a few critical topics:

- To retain your visitors devoted to your business, engage them with your content.
- Create links to bring people to your site in the first place.

If you follow these two procedures every time, your audience will locate your site, return to it, and refer their friends to you. Your achievement will then "snowball," right? Yes, to some extent, but additional work still needs to be done. You, like everything else in business, must be "special." You must put something valuable and fascinating out there. This is the moment to progress from "good" to "great" content development. This is the only method to attain your desired results.

What Characterizes Great Content

Great content is simple. It beneficially engages most of your target audience while increasing your exposure and profitability. But what magical components are required to create amazing content?

Content is simply information. The information may be intended to teach, entertain, or persuade. However, when it is "great" content, it achieves its purpose while also assisting you in growing your business. It is successful in two ways. Review the following general characteristics to help you understand what constitutes exceptional content:

Your Audience Can Find Your Content Easily

All of your research, careful writing and editing, multiple retakes of the video, and effort spent preparing your content are useless if no one can find it. You must ensure that the people you want to read it can do so. To accomplish this, emphasize it on your website and ensure it appears in a search engine query. The easiest way to achieve the latter is to employ relevant keywords and ensure your content is optimized for such terms.

Furthermore, having a well-organized "library" on your site might assist your readers in finding your information. Plus, Google appreciates a well-organized library! Sitemaps, navigation menus, and breadcrumbs are all excellent ways to organize your site and assist users in finding what they are looking for. Search bars are also useful additions to your website. It makes it simple for users to access further content on a specific topic or to return to something they previously watched.

Offering a section or sidebar of your "best" material is another fantastic feature to consider to increase your findability. Emphasize your most popular content and material. This encourages viewers to stay longer and engage more with your content. Another useful component is one for displaying new content.

This might be on your homepage or another frequently visited page. You can also promote new material by emailing your mailing list when it is published on your website.

Your Audience Can Easily Share Your Content

Great content is something that people want to share, as well as something that they can share. Start with a great message to ensure your material is shareable and people want to share it. Make sure you want to share this knowledge if you come across it. It's probably not the proper message if you're not excited about it or are even embarrassed to share it. Spend a lot of effort on the framework of your essay as well. This refers to the "cover" of your content, the elements that people notice before engaging with the message's body. Consider the image that people will view initially, as well as the tagline and headline. Anything that people will notice first should be carefully considered. You will lose clicks and shares if these elements do not capture attention.

Embed share features in your content to make it easier to share. Share buttons, social buttons, and links that allow your audience to tweet your material make spreading your message a breeze easily. Make sure you give the sharing opportunity a fair go. Consider phrases like "stupidly simple" or "no effort," and make sure your audience understands how simple it is for them to share your information and move on. If you make it too difficult for your audience, such as requiring them to copy and paste links or headlines to tweet your message, your material better be worth it (and that level of quality is difficult to achieve)!

Your Audience Can Use Your Content

Your material must not just add value to the lives of your target audience, but it must also be consumable. It must be simple to understand and interact with.

For example, if you design your website to be simple to use and comprehend, the information you add will most likely be simple to use. The important words in the previous phrase are "most likely." You must continue to consider usability with each piece of material you create. If you create a tool or app or want your audience to do something, you must ensure that it is useable content.

For example, suppose you construct an app or design an online tool. In that case, you must first test it with users, collect their input, make the required modifications to improve it, and then advertise it (or conduct another usability test). You must conduct due diligence and be confident that your material can be used in various contexts, browsers, etc. Make sure to test it out on a mobile device as well. What is the content's load time?

Your Audience Can Easily Read Your Content

But what if your content isn't a tool or app? What if your material is in the form of text? How do you ensure that it is usable? Check that the audience can read it! This encompasses both good writing and design. Check that the font is large enough on the screen, that the text color contrasts with the backdrop, and that the background is not too distracting.

Adjust the column width so readers can easily track where they are in the column and the leading, or line spacing, is not too tight. Among the methods for making your text more readable are:

- Lists (like this one!)- information that is easy to scan and that you want your reader to remember.

- Clear and succinct words and paragraphs--do not ramble and write as if you were expressing the topic (with proper grammar).

- Easy-to-find chunks- bulleted lists and headings/subheadings are wonderful ways to make information stand out while scanning. Consider things like bolding or enlarging essential quotes or information.

Your Audience Can Remember Your Content

Your content should be "sticky," meaning the material should stick with the audience members once they interact with it. To make it "stickier," answer the following question: "So what?" Take a stand or make a link no one else has thought about. Be unique.

Your Audience Can Quote Your Content

Consider each line an opportunity to provide your audience with a "soundbite." It is funny and only has 140 characters. Writing every line this way would be tedious, but there is an opportunity to be quoted on something valuable! When you get quoted, your content becomes more memorable and shareable. Consider the following to help you enhance your work so that it is more easily quoted:

- Read a lot of quality writing. Copy the writing style of writers you admire until you find your own. Do not limit yourself to only reading online work; also read newspapers, magazines, and books.

- Rework sentences to make them as short as feasible. Remember that clarity and conciseness are crucial characteristics of successful writing.

- When appropriate, use humor. Don't try to be funny in your work if you're not naturally funny. Instead, make a statement with your brilliance, wit, or poignancy.

- Demonstrate to your readers what is quotable. Remove the guesswork by emphasizing the quotable content. Make it bold or place it in a text box so your audience can notice it quickly.

- Avoid the "cliche" "trap" (wink): Make sure your audience is quoting your genius, not someone else's. You don't want people to use an overused cliché to quote you.

Your Audience Can Act On Your Content

One of the numerous reasons to publish content is to position yourself as an expert on a particular topic. When people are looking for assistance or an answer, and you offer your expertise for free, they will appreciate and trust your company. This trust will drive them to return to your site and possibly choose you over your competitors. The ideal instructional content is crafted so your audience can act on it. It indicates they believe they have the capacity and talents to do everything you tell them to do. Furthermore, you want them to feel compelled to act immediately now. Consider adding phrases like "....you can experiment with today" or "use X to get Y right away" to your headlines and posts.

Your Audience Can Provide Reportable Data

Make a goal for each piece of material you produce. You are likely to have overlapping and multiple goals for diverse content strategies. Just make sure you know what you want to gain from it and how you will determine whether or not you are successful. This is why reporting tools are essential. Some common objectives to examine are:

- **Conversion**: Are viewers and readers becoming hot leads and, eventually, sales?

- **Engagement**: Do your audience members share your material, leave comments on your videos or articles, spend a lot of time on your pages, and check your emails?

40

- **Traffic**: This is the most straightforward approach for tracking and reporting. It is keeping track of how many people visit your website. This information is not valuable in and of itself, but it is useful to know.

Using these statistics and analytics, you can determine whether or not the content is effective, and you can also use your most data-backed, successful content pieces as templates to develop more in the future. This allows you to repeat what you know works while avoiding what does not.

Why Do You Post Where You Post?

The context of your communications, as well as the assets you have, dictate how and where you should sell your material. If your website and business are already well-known, you may not need to advertise your material as aggressively, but if you want to increase your visibility, you must work more to get your content out there. You may need to devote more time to promotion than you did to creation!

Here are some locations you should think about submitting your content:

1. **Reddit**: an excellent place to have a dialogue, but be cautious about how you advertise your knowledge. It must not appear to be spam or fluff. Only articles and stuff with high value.

2. **Medium**: a website where you can republish blog posts or parts of whole articles. If you only advertise a piece of a longer story, send viewers to your website for further information.

3. **Email**: While this is a "tried and true" mode of communication, it is still an excellent approach to keep readers engaged with new content consistently. Email readers are three times more likely than social

media users to share content and six times more likely to click on links within it.

4. **Twitter**: personal and branded: If your piece or material is related to your brand, share it on your brand's profile, but also consider promoting it on your personal profile. Because of the speed of the social networking site, having multiple locations is beneficial—just space out your shares so your followers aren't overwhelmed. The same applies to using Twitter conversations; hashtag-relevant chats should be used selectively, not to overwhelm followers.

5. **Facebook**: personal and professional: Personal pages are a terrific area to exchange content, but you may be concerned that your content will bother your friends and family. If this is the case, create a list of only professional contacts so that your family and personal acquaintances are not exposed to your content marketing communications. If your content is important to your brand, you can create a post on Facebook that includes a meaningful quotation from the content, a strong image, and a link back to the entire message. A Facebook Group is another option to examine. This venue is ideal for disseminating industry-related content to a big, engaged group. To remain relevant but not overpowering, share your content no more than once a month. You can publish and respond to other people's posts more frequently as long as you're contributing valuable discourse.

6. **LinkedIn Articles and Groups**: Disseminate your content on your personal LinkedIn profile. As an added advantage, Google will not consider this a duplicate post, so you will gain greater traction. LinkedIn also has an in-built system for notifying users of new posts from individuals they follow, so your readers will be notified without you having to do anything additional. Groups, which are similar to

Facebook groups, allow you to share industry-related content. Simply make sure you read the group's policies and participate positively.

7. **Pinterest**: Make your boards public and allow others to contribute stuff to a topic. This is an excellent way to increase traffic and learn about your target audience.

8. **Instagram**: Include only a snippet of your content on Instagram, along with a strong photograph, a caption, and a link to the entire content. You can also create a tale with a one-day lifespan to help disseminate your content.

9. **YouTube**: If your material isn't a video, consider making one about it! Have someone discuss the main points of your post or eBook. Talk about the findings in your whitepaper. You can still use this media even if your primary source is something else. Remember to include a link back to your original and comprehensive content message.

Prepare to Write!

Decide on a Theme for Your Essay

This may be the most difficult phase, but if you have completed the steps in the previous chapters, you should have a decent notion of where to begin. However, you can become trapped at times. This is why it is a good idea always to keep a list of potential topics in mind. Consider the following to refresh old concepts:

- Explain how two seemingly unrelated ideas are linked.
- Convert a "How To" to a "How Not To."
- Create a "Next Steps" follow-up post to a post you have or have not yet created.

Complete Your Homework

Once you have an idea, you must gather facts. What has already been written about the subject? What has gained popularity? What medium was employed, and how are you evaluating its effectiveness? Use the following as a starting point for your research:

- How about the format, length, heading, scanability, readability, and so on?
- What draws your attention to the title?
- What keywords are consumers using to find your content? What are they searching for on Google?
- How are social media platforms used?
- What are the top keywords?
- How unique is your viewpoint compared to other articles on the subject?
- What images are employed? What is the format?
- How can you create links?
- What are the followers' comments? Do they have any additional questions, or do they have a favorite section of the content?

Look for items that are missing as well. Also, give your thoughts some time to percolate. Take some time to reflect on what you're writing and why you're writing it.

It's Writing Time!

It is time to write after you have completed an extensive investigation. Plan out how you'll write it, and then do it! Maybe you plan first and then write later, or maybe you plan and write right away. Discover what works best for you. You might also create a content formula, such as:

- Title and subheadings
- Problem identification
- Research undertaken
- Revelation and call to action

Distribute Your Content

As previously stated, you must distribute your material where it is relevant and connected with your strengths. Follow the recommendations to ensure that you get it where it needs to be in the format that works for that platform.

Set out time in your calendar for this Quick Start Action Step to tackle one step at a time until you have a terrific piece ready to be sold on relevant sites. But don't post anything yet! Simply have it ready!

SEO AND CONTENT OPTIMIZATION

S earch engine optimization entails naturally increasing the rank of a website in search engine results through non-paid tactics to have the site rank as high as feasible. A search engine is a website that searches the Internet for results based on keywords or key phrases the user enters. Simply put, whatever you type into a search engine returns results from the web that it believes are relevant to your query. Yahoo and Bing are two more search engines in addition to Google.

How do search engines function? Search engines can return results by crawling, indexing, and retrieving.

During crawling, robots, also known as spiders, examine websites for information and data such as page titles, image tags, headings, content, keywords utilized, and more.

Because crawlers perform this, it is automated and fast. Indexing is collecting all the data discovered throughout the crawling process. Retrieving entails providing the user with the most accurate results from the site pages crawled concerning the search query entered.

Let me use an example to explain the power of search engines. Enter the term' auto dealer' into Google. Google returns 170 million results! Despite this,

Google could rank all 170 million of those sites and even choose one to rank first. How did it come to that conclusion?

Google has a broad number of ranking variables, including:

- Keywords used
- Image optimization
- Inbound and outbound links
- Domain age and authority
- Social shares

These are only a few of the most important. There are about 100 such ranking variables, with a complete online list. However, remember that the industry prepares the lists of ranking variables rather than Google. Google has never disclosed a list of its ranking variables, citing frequent changes in its ranking algorithm as the cause.

SEO efforts can be divided into three categories:

- On-page SEO
- Off-page SEO
- Local SEO

On-page SEO deals with everything you do on your business site, off-page SEO deals with what you do on other sites, and local SEO encompasses both on-site and off-site (though largely off-site) efforts to improve rankings in local search results.

On-page SEO

On-page SEO entails making efforts on the site, such as using relevant keywords and having a solid site structure. This mostly entails utilizing relevant keywords throughout the site content and maintaining a tidy site layout. On-page elements that must be optimized include title tags, meta descriptions, headers, page content, and picture alt text. This is accomplished by incorporating keywords that you wish to rank for throughout the article.

On-page SEO also entails maintaining a clean site layout that is simple for search engine crawlers to scan and index. Because on-page occurs on your site, you have complete control, making it simple. Because it is so simple, most sites have great on-page SEO, making it less significant on rankings. That doesn't imply it's unimportant. It simply implies that almost everyone has their on-page SEO down pat; thus, depending just on on-page strategies will not help you stand out in front of search engines.

Popular on-page SEO tools include Yoast SEO (for WordPress), Moz On-Page Grader, and SEMrush's On-Page SEO Checker.

Off-page SEO

Off-page SEO is harder to master and requires more time and effort for businesses. Off-page, as the name implies, occurs on external sites, with decisions made by third parties. Off-page SEO consists primarily of two activities: obtaining incoming links from external sites referring to your site and obtaining social shares of your site's content.

Even though social shares are a big element of social media, social signals like your content being socially shared are valuable to search engines and part of off-page optimization. Off-page SEO informs search engines about how your site compares to others. Each link to your site and social share of your site's content is a vote of approval from others. And the more you have, the better you will appear in search engines. Of course, many factors matter, such as the quality and relevance of the sites that link to you, as detailed below.

Local SEO

Local SEO is critical for businesses with a physical address or those targeting a specific geographical region. If your company has a physical location, local SEO can help you rank in search results for queries made near your business and make you visible to searchers in your region, putting you in front of potential clients based on their location. You've probably come across local search results while searching for a product or service and have the results come up with a map or list of local businesses that provide that product or service and are located in your area.

Local SEO is responsible for search results that are close to you. For businesses with a local presence, local SEO tools like Moz Local and Google My Business provide insights into local search performance and help you manage your business information across various platforms.

On-page SEO is just concerned with methods on your site's pages; it has nothing to do with other sites. It consists of two components:

- Optimizing: This is done by inserting keywords into the page text, headings, title tags, meta descriptions, etc. The keywords used are the ones you want to rank for when people search for them. Keywords are chosen depending on their traffic and competitiveness, a process known as keyword research.

- Having a clear and easy-to-navigate site structure

Site Structure

It is critical to get your site structure right. The organization, storage, and presentation of your site's material influences not just its user-friendliness but also the ability of search engines to identify and index your site. A clean and well-structured website is easier for search engines to find and read, increasing your crawl rate and enhancing your chances of ranking.

The basis of your site and the first and most significant stage is its structure. If this phase is not followed correctly, no matter how good your content is, it will be useless if the site structure is poor. A decent site structure is at the heart of effective SEO.

Make certain that your website is not invisible to search engines. If the site structure is not legible by site crawlers, the site may become invisible to search engines. How do you avoid or eliminate this problem?

- Increase the number of links on your website by interlinking your pages.
- Make a sitemap and submit it to Google Search Central.
- Make a sitemap for your readers on your own website. This one refers to the one developed for users instead of the one created for Google Search Central.

How can you tell if search engines are crawling and indexing your site?

- Try it out with Google.
- Enter site:domain.com into Google.
- Enter it without the http or www.

When you type the above into Google, it will tell you how many results it found. As I write this, the above search yields' 2 results' because the site only has the home page and an about page and hasn't officially launched yet. What matters is that Google returns results for the above search query, and your site should do the same.

Consider the following when designing your website's structure:

- Choosing the structure of your menu (navigation)
- The number of dropdowns in the navigation
- Permalink structures
- The internal linking structure

How to Create an Effective Website Structure

- Have a well-organized framework that is simple to traverse for your guests.
- Include a home page button on all pages visitors can use to navigate to deeper pages on your site.
- Avoid overcomplicating the hierarchy of your navigation bar. A large number of dropdown menus will confuse the user.
- Create a descriptive URL structure that illustrates your structure and will be followed by all your permalinks. For example, if your company has many locations, change the URL structure to example.com/locations/toronto rather than example.com/toronto.
- Instead of using JavaScript, create your site's navigation and content with HTML or CSS.
- Create an internal connection structure.
- Rather than removing pages and issuing 404s, redirect them with 301s.

Performing Keyword Research

The first and most critical step in optimization is keyword research. All of your SEO efforts should revolve around the keywords you select. Optimizing without keywords is analogous to strategizing without objectives. The keywords you select are the ones for which you want to rank. They must be picked with care, investigation, and data to back up your selection.

Keyword research is more than just picking a lot of keywords that are relevant to you and cramming them into your web pages. Yes, relevancy is crucial, but so are numbers. You should investigate how much traffic those keywords receive and how difficult it is to rank them. Some keywords are highly relevant but extremely difficult to rank for, so pursuing them may not always be the best option. Spend your time and energy on less competitive keywords.

Some questions to consider when selecting keywords are:

- Are the keywords you've chosen being searched frequently enough to obtain good traffic from them if you rank?
- Will the terms you choose be easy to rank for, or will they require months, if not years, of effort to appear?
- Is there enough traffic from the locations where your product or service is sold?
- Are the keywords pertinent to your industry?

How did you learn all of this? Sign in to AdWords.Adwords.google.ca/ KeywordPlanner is the URL for the Google Keyword Planner tool. It will provide you with detailed information about your chosen keywords, such as their competitiveness level and search volume.

Steps To Take While Conducting Keyword Research

Note all the keywords and key phrases that come to mind. There are several approaches you can take. Make a comprehensive list of keywords relevant to your business that customers may enter into search engines to find businesses like yours. Make a list of key terms that are variations on those keywords.

Expand your list by using alternative ways to phrase the same thing (use synonyms).

For example, if you own a high-end jewelry business, some of the keywords that instantly come to mind are:

- gold jewelry
- platinum jewelry
- silver jewelry
- diamond jewelry

These are only the most important core keywords. When you add more information, you get:

- gold jewelry shop
- platinum jewelry shop
- silver jewelry shop
- diamond jewelry shop

With even more information, you get key phrases like 'purchase gold jewelry online' and so on for platinum, silver, etc. You may also use location modifiers to get 'gold jewelry store Toronto' and so on. You may also duplicate your keychains by replacing 'jewelry' with 'jewelry.'

They are simply two distinct spellings of the same term in different nations. Investigate such modifiers. You can even go longtail and create them through questions like "Where can I buy gold jewelry?" You can also include searches for extra services you provide or topics you believe people may be interested in, such as 'where to have jewelry fixed,' 'ring cleaning,' and so on.

My most important recommendation is to put yourself in the customer's shoes and think from their point of view. In this scenario, you'd ask yourself, "If I were a customer looking for a jewelry store in Toronto, what are all the possible search queries I could enter into a search engine to find what I'm looking for?"

If you've run out of ideas, you can use keyword suggestion programs such as Ubersuggest (ubersuggest.org). Here's an extra tip: utilize Google Suggest. Google suggests a list of ideas displayed at the bottom of the search results page and based on previous searches.

Then, enter all the terms into Google Keyword Planner, which may be found at adwords.google.ca/Key-wordPlanner.

The Adwords keyword planner is intended for selecting keywords for your pay-per-click campaign, but it also provides information for selecting keywords for on-page SEO. Enter your search terms into the tool, and it will provide information such as search volume, keyword ideas, and ranking competitiveness.

You're mostly looking for golden possibilities here: keywords with a high search volume but low to medium-ranking competition.

These keywords will be easier to rank and have enough search traffic to be worth the effort. This will be easier to perform in an Excel spreadsheet, so import your results and arrange your spreadsheet. It's worth noting that the keyword competition score in the tool is for paid ranks. Therefore, getting a more realistic score for organic search results from a keyword difficulty tool is best. It is generally similar in most cases because a term that is difficult to rank for through pay-per-click is usually difficult to rank for organically as well, so begin by using the Adwords term Planner.

After entering all your brainstorming keywords into the tool and selecting the best combination of high search traffic and low to medium competition, save the results in Excel format. Choose your major and secondary keywords from your final chosen keyword, depending on the numbers. Your major keyword is the one you want to rank for and believe will bring you the most business if you rank for it. The principal keyword will be used in the content on your main pages, such as the home page, and other essential pages, such as the About page, service page, and so on. Because they are the most powerful sites, your primary keywords should be used in their text. Secondary keywords will be employed in the material on less powerful pages, such as blog content pages. You're ready to optimize once you've matched your keywords with suitable sites based on their significance.

Content Optimization for Your Website

Once you've selected which pages you want to rank for specific keywords, i.e., which keywords you want to utilize on which pages, incorporate the keywords into the page's text across the following on-page elements:

- Title tag*
- Meta description tag
- Meta tags
- Article title/Page Title*
- Content Headings
- In the content material
- URL of the page
- Image description and Alt text
- Article tags

*Note that the page/article title and title tag are distinct. They are both page titles, but the title tag is displayed in search results, and the page/article title is displayed on your site. You can keep them both the same or slightly alter them.

Get a good SEO plugin for your CMS to add keywords to the title tag, meta tags, and meta description. The Yoast SEO plugin for WordPress is a nice one, and it can be found at wordpress.org/plugins/wordpress-seo. After installing the plugin, you'll see a place for each page's tags and descriptions.

The title tag will appear as the header at the top of your listing in search engine results, and the meta description will appear beneath it. People see this when they see your website ranking in search results and determine whether or not to click on it. Therefore, they must be original, educational, useful, and compelling to receive the most hits.

In addition to the initial, keep in mind the content's keyword density and aim to insert the keywords in the first 100 words at the very least. The keyword density is the percentage of times the term appears in the body of the material based on the total number of words. Try to keep the density between 2% and 3% and make it look as natural as possible by not repeating your term too many times. It is critical to develop content first and foremost for your reader and then for search engine ranking considerations.

Suppose you simply repeat your keyword in your content for ranking purposes. In that case, your content will become unusable to the reader, and they will close your page immediately, spending less time on your site, which Google interprets as your page being unusable and lowers your rankings. As a result, keyword stuffing will backfire on you. Try to improve your page load times, which is another search engine ranking consideration.

The SEO plugin optimizes the page title, meta tags, and meta description; your CMS handles the rest. You can utilize your keywords in picture descriptions, alt text, page content, and so on while working in your CMS as usual.

Keeping Penalties at Bay

Read Google Search Central guidelines and follow them to avoid being penalized. The standards include basic criteria such as not writing low-quality content, not publishing duplicate content, not writing thin content, not keyword stuffing, and more.

How to Tell If You've Received a Penalty

You may face two types of punishments: *manual penalties* and *algorithmic penalties*.

If you are subjected to a manual penalty by Google's staff, you will receive a notification in your Google Search Central account. Manual penalties occur when a member of Google's webspam prevention department discovers that you have violated any of Google's guidelines and manually reports you to the system. You've been slapped with a manual penalty if you receive a notification in your Google Search Central account.

Algorithmic penalties, on the other hand, affect all websites and occur whenever Google changes how websites are ranked, i.e., when an algorithm is updated. You'll know if you've been penalized if you see a decline in traffic and rankings. It's a good idea to use tools like Rank Tracker (moz.com/tools/rank-tracker) and Positionly (positionly.com) to keep track of your ranking positions.

What to Do If You've Received a Penalty

Based on what you've been penalized for, either disavow or reconsiderations are the answer. You can disavow backlinks that you believe are of poor quality and are affecting your site's rating. Disavowing links does not erase them, but it does inform Google not to consider them when evaluating your site. A reconsideration request asks Google to investigate your site after you've taken steps to address the issues identified in the manual action notification in Google Search Central.

Disavow Procedure

Disavow links with Google Disavow. You must first download all of your links, then select the ones you want to disavow, and finally, upload a list of only the ones you want to disavow. This document must be in.txt format and posted to your web admin's area's search console. The list of disavowed links must be supplied in a specified format, which looks like this: domain:example.com. The links you intend to disavow will most likely include sites with different formats, such as http:// or www.

Process of Reconsideration

As previously stated, reconsideration petitions are exclusively for manual penalties, for which you will receive a notification in your Search Console account. Before submitting a reconsideration request, make sure you've made the necessary changes and resolved the issue that prompted the manual punishment.

When you're ready to submit the request, go to your Search Console account and click manual actions' under search traffic' in the left-hand sidebar. Click the 'request a review' button and attach your reconsideration request paper. This document must be in.txt format and prepared in a fashion comparable to an email or letter, with details on the effort made to resolve the problem.

Begin the document by explaining why the punishment was imposed and what steps were taken to correct it. Then, go into greater depth about the efforts done to resolve the issue and offer evidence. Proof can be provided by putting information in a Google document or spreadsheet in Google Drive and linking to it. However, ensure that your sheet access is set to public so that they may view it.

This sheet can include a list of links that have been removed or pages on your site that have been fixed, among other things. Provide all required information on the proof sheet, but keep the reconsideration document brief. Remember that this will be read by a human from the Google webpam team, not a computer, so don't make it too long. Also, tell them what you intend to do in the future and how you intend to avoid making the same mistake again. Making it appear that it is Google's fault, being nasty, rambling on and on about how the penalty has damaged you and begging for forgiveness are all things you should avoid.

SEO Q&A

Do I need SEO?

Hundreds of thousands see a high ranking in search results, which is critical for bringing in traffic and leads, both of which are critical for any business. So, yes, you do require SEO. The higher you rank in search engines, the more clicks you get to your site and the more traffic you get, which leads to more sales.

Is it better to pay someone or do it myself?

SEO can sometimes be frightening, and whether you can manage it depends on your learning curve, competition, situation, and available time. Larger corporations are more likely to pay SEOs to perform everything for them. If you own a small firm, it may not be feasible. However, it is not impossible. Over time, you should be able to learn it all and have your site rank higher by implementing tactics, measuring results, and making modifications depending on them. The fundamentals are straightforward, but issues such as penalties can complicate matters. Seek professional assistance if you are facing a penalty.

How long will it take to reach the top?

SEO efforts can take some time to bear fruit. It all depends on who is outranking you and the strength of their website. For certain keywords, the sites outranking you will be far more powerful, and ranking for those keywords can take months, if not a year. Less competitive terms, on the other hand, may require a few days to a few weeks of effort. To determine your core keywords' competitiveness, look at who ranks for them, examine their site metrics and backlinks, and then compare it all to your site to see how it compares.

What distinguishes SEO from SEM?

SEO entails making organic attempts to rank in search engines, whereas SEM entails paid efforts such as PPC in addition to ranking organically. In a nutshell, SEM is SEO plus PPC.

How do search engines function, and how do they rank?

Search engines use robots (also known as spiders) to crawl websites and record their content as they scan them. This is all done incredibly quickly, and it has to be done quickly because there are so many sites to go through. Sites are graded on relevancy and usefulness based on the information discovered by robots and a range of other variables. Tools like SEMrush, Ahrefs, and SERPWatcher offer rank-tracking features.

How does Google discover my site?

Google can find your website in a variety of ways. When you first launch your site, a recommended practice is to submit your site URL to search engines personally. Creating a sitemap also assists Google in discovering deeper pages on your site. Backlinks from other sites also aid in discovering and crawling your content.

Why isn't my website appearing on Google?

If you have a new website, the reason it isn't showing up on Google is most likely because the search robots haven't crawled it yet. Google crawls a new website, or even an existing one with new modifications, in about ten days on average. Manually submit your site to Google Search Console to expedite the process. It is doubtful that sites that have been online for a time will not appear in search results. One possibility is that the site is so far behind in the rankings that manually determining the rank number is impossible.

In that scenario, enter your site and a few keywords into rank tracking tools (links to them may be found on the tools page), and they will tell you which page your site is on. Sometimes, your site could be hundreds of pages deep in the search results, making it impossible to find manually. This does not imply that your website is not listed on Google. It's just very behind in terms of results.

Why isn't my website listed on Google anymore?

You may have lost rankings due to a penalty or seen a dip in rankings. Remember that a decline in rankings is not the same as getting completely removed from the results. Enter your site and the keywords you're no longer ranking for into rank checker programs like Positionly and Rank Tracker to see whether you're no longer ranking for the keyword or ranking very late.

If you no longer rank for them, examine your Google Analytics account to see if there has been a significant decrease in traffic, and check your Google Search Console account for any notifications or messages indicating a penalty.

You've most likely received a penalty. If you're still ranking but have been pushed down, it's most likely due to a low click-through rate, a high bounce rate, or other sites suddenly becoming more relevant for the phrase than you due to on-page optimization or an increase in backlinks.

What is the distinction between crawling and indexing?

Simply put, crawling is the process of finding information, while indexing is the act of storing information. Crawling, indexing, and retrieving are the three basic phases that search engines take. Crawling occurs when search engine robots visit pages and study their content; indexing occurs when information about specific words and material and their location is preserved; and retrieving occurs when Google algorithms look up the search terms in the index and deliver appropriate results.

SOCIAL MEDIA CONTENT STRATEGY

Social media marketing entails promoting your company on social media platforms, allowing users to generate and share information and network with one another. Social media is not like most marketing platforms. Traditionally, social media was not intended to be a marketing tool but rather a platform for ordinary people to interact and network. It gradually transformed into a marketing tool for business owners. Compared to other marketing channels, such as radio and publications, social media is the only platform where consumers create content. It is a community-like, consumer-centric platform from which you can obtain so much if you understand your target well.

Social media platforms provide an opportunity to broaden your reach and raise brand awareness. Assume there was a huge event coming up with millions of attendees, and you were granted the opportunity to speak or set up a stall for free. You'd never pass up an opportunity like that, would you? That is what social media stands for. An online real-time event with millions of visitors where you may set up your stall, in this case, your profile, for free. It's too good to pass up.

Platforms for Social Media Marketing

Facebook

- Users: Facebook has 2.989 billion monthly active users.
- Audience: A balanced mix of Generation X and Millennials.
- Industry impact: B2C industry
- Best for: Brand recognition; advertising
- Content Style: Facebook content can range from informative to entertaining. Use a mix of text, images, videos, and links.
- Engagement: Encourage likes, shares, and comments by asking questions, sharing relatable stories, and using eye-catching visuals.
- Video: Native videos and live streams tend to perform well on Facebook. Use captions for videos since many users watch videos without sound.

Facebook is the most popular and well-established social networking platform. Since its inception in 2004, it has proven to be a vital resource for B2C enterprises, providing complex advertising capabilities and organic prospects.

TikTok

- Users: TikTok has 1 billion active monthly users worldwide.
- Audience: Gen Z is the primary target audience, followed by Millennials.
- Industry impact: B2B and B2C industry
- Best for: innovative, short-form video material; user-generated content; brand awareness
- Short-Form Video: TikTok is all about short, creative videos. Keep them engaging, entertaining, and authentic.

- Trending Challenges: Participate in trending challenges to increase visibility.
- Music and Effects: Utilize the platform's music and effects to add a unique touch to your videos.

TikTok is arguably the first thing that comes to mind when considering short-form videos. The platform's popularity skyrocketed in 2020 and shows no signs of abating. It's one of the best sites for developing communities, with marketers putting it second only to YouTube.

Instagram

- Users: Instagram has 2 billion monthly active users.
- Audience: Millennials.
- Industry impact: B2C industry
- Best for: High-quality photos and videos, user-generated content, and advertising
- Visual Focus: Instagram is highly visual. High-quality images, aesthetically pleasing graphics, and short videos are key.
- Hashtags: Use relevant and popular hashtags to increase discoverability.
- Stories and Reels: Utilize Instagram Stories for behind-the-scenes content and Reels for short, engaging videos.
- Engagement: Engage with your audience by responding to comments and using interactive features like polls, quizzes, and questions.

Even though Instagram was only created 12 years ago, it has taken the world by storm. Instagram is where marketers go when it comes to sharing visually appealing content. Another feature that distinguishes the platform is its advanced e-commerce features. Users may now discover brands, peruse their products and services, and make a purchase without ever leaving the app, making Instagram a difficult platform to compete with.

Twitter

- Users: Twitter has 372.9 million monthly active users throughout the world.
- Audience: Millennials.
- Industry impact: B2B and B2C industry
- Best for: public relations, customer service, and community development
- Brevity: Twitter's character limit encourages concise and to-the-point content.
- Timeliness: Tweet about current events and trending topics to stay relevant.
- Visuals: Include images, GIFs, and videos to make your tweets more engaging.
- Hashtags: Use relevant hashtags to expand your reach and join conversations.

While Instagram emphasizes pictures, Twitter emphasizes words. Since the days of 140-character Tweets, the platform has grown to include an audio tool called Twitter Spaces, a community-building tool called Twitter Communities, and Twitter Moments, which allows you to share fascinating items with your followers.

LinkedIn

- Users: 774 million active LinkedIn users worldwide
- Audience: Baby boomers, Generation X, and Millennials.
- Industry impact: B2B industry
- Best for: B2B partnerships, business development, and social selling
- Professional Tone: LinkedIn is a professional platform, so focus on industry insights, thought leadership, and networking.

- Long-Form Content: Publish longer posts and articles to share in-depth insights.
- Visuals: Use professional images and graphics. LinkedIn's carousel feature can showcase multiple visuals in one post.
- Engagement: Encourage meaningful discussions by posing thought-provoking questions.

LinkedIn is the professional cousin of Facebook. It's possibly the only platform with a clearly defined audience: working professionals eager to network and find new possibilities. As a result, it is great for B2B organizations wishing to identify key decision-makers and develop an industry-specific network.

YouTube

- Users: YouTube has around 315 million daily active users throughout the world.
- Audience: Primarily Millennials, but has a strong audience across gender and age demographics.
- Industry impact: B2C and B2B
- Best for: Brand recognition, long-form entertainment, and how-to videos
- Video Content: YouTube is a video-centric platform. Create informative, educational, and entertaining videos.
- SEO: Optimize video titles, descriptions, and tags for search visibility.
- Consistency: Maintain a regular uploading schedule to build a loyal subscriber base.

YouTube is the world's second most viewed website, according to Hootsuite. Furthermore, marketers regard it as the finest platform for community building. In addition to being a very popular network, its users prefer to stay on it for longer because it offers long-form content, making it a great medium for sharing educational content.

Snapchat

- Users: 750 million monthly active users worldwide
- Audience: Gen Z.
- Industry impact: B2C industry
- Best for: Brand recognition; advertising
- Ephemeral Content: Snapchat content disappears after a short time. Use it for real-time updates and behind-the-scenes content.
- Lenses and Filters: Incorporate interactive lenses and filters for playful engagement.

Snapchat was the pioneer in ephemeral content when it launched in 2011. It introduced content that could be shared with friends but would expire after 24 hours. The platform reached its pinnacle in 2015 and has been stable since then. Many people assumed the brand would vanish when Instagram debuted Stories, a similar function with a different name. Snapchat, on the other hand, remains popular among young adults.

Pinterest

- Users: Pinterest has 463 million monthly active users worldwide.
- Audience: Primarily Millennials, with a sizable contingent of Gen Z, Gen X, and Baby Boomers.
- Industry impact: B2C industry
- Best for: visual advertisement; inspiration
- Visual Discovery: Pinterest is a visual search engine. Create eye-catching, long vertical pins with compelling graphics.

- How-Tos and DIYs: Share tutorials, guides, and DIY content that aligns with your brand
- Keyword Optimization: Use descriptive titles and keywords to improve discoverability.

Consider Pinterest a visual storyboard where users can find inspiration for anything from fashion to home decor. Pinterest is where 85% of Pinners go to start a new project. Furthermore, 80% of weekly Pinners say they've discovered a new company or product on Pinterest. As a result, it is a terrific discovery tool and allows companies to develop their narrative through visual stories.

Clubhouse

- Users: 10 million weekly active users globally
- Audience: Millennials are the primary target audience.
- Industry impact: B2B and B2C
- Best for: visual advertisement; inspiration
- Audio Conversations: Clubhouse is focused on audio discussions and conversations.
- Participation: Join rooms, moderate discussions, and share your insights.
- Networking: Use Clubhouse to connect with professionals, share expertise, and engage in niche topics.
- Value: Provide valuable insights and contribute to meaningful conversations.

Clubhouse made an immediate impact when it first appeared on social media in 2020. The audio-only platform enables people to initiate intriguing discussions with followers and strangers alike, allowing them to establish a community. The platform also drew attention for its invitation-only setup when it was in beta testing. The platform is now available worldwide and on both IOS and Android smartphones. Another major selling feature of this platform is that it works well for both B2B and B2C enterprises and uses audio, which has made a significant comeback in recent years.

Now that we've covered the basics of each social media platform, let's talk about why social media marketing is valuable to your business.

Benefits of Social Media Marketing:

Social media marketing has emerged as a dynamic and indispensable strategy for companies of all sizes and industries. It's not merely a trend; it's a powerful tool that offers many benefits to businesses seeking to thrive in the competitive online landscape.

The journey into social media marketing unfolds a world of opportunities – the chance to reach a global audience, engage in real-time conversations, and craft compelling narratives that resonate with individuals on a personal level. As we navigate the diverse advantages that social media marketing offers, it becomes clear that its potential to elevate businesses to new heights is both undeniable and limitless.

There are numerous reasons why your business should employ social media marketing. We've compiled a list of the most compelling reasons to think about.

Raise Your Brand's Visibility

Because of the sheer number of individuals on social media, if you don't have a presence, you're missing out on the opportunity to reach thousands, if not millions, of people. In fact, social media has been shown to increase brand exposure through increasing engagement. Comments, likes, shares, reposts, and saves are examples of social interaction. It also aids in brand exposure by

DIGITAL MARKETING CONTENT CREATION

directing traffic directly to your website. To accomplish this, include connections to your website and other offers in your profile, bio, and posts.

Increase Lead Generation and Conversions

Because you're advertising to individuals who have chosen to engage with you by following your account, promoting and sharing your items on social media is a straightforward approach to improving lead generation, boosting conversions, and increasing sales.

Here are some ideas for how to use social media to create more leads.

- Create contests on your social media profiles for your visitors and followers to enter.
- Include links to your website and offerings in the bio part of your profiles.
- Host live videos to make product introductions and share updates or specifics about exciting corporate news.
- Launch a social media marketing campaign through one of your platforms.

Use your social profiles to sell your stuff. For example, you can enable Facebook's Shop Section or Instagram's Shopping function on your profiles. These capabilities allow your visitors and followers to access details such as price, material, and size by clicking on products you've featured in posts. Then, visitors may quickly proceed to the platform's checkout and purchase the product straight from you.

Develop Ties With Your Clients

You may develop long-lasting relationships with your social media followers by interacting and engaging with them. You can accomplish this by connecting with them through your postings, responding to their questions and comments, and offering assistance. You can also ask your followers questions about your products and their problems or organize giveaways to help you build trust and demonstrate how much you appreciate their feedback and support.

Study Your Competitors

Social media is an excellent tool for monitoring your competitors' social media strategies, marketing items, campaigns they're running, and the amount of contact with followers. Social media allows you to see what is and isn't working for your competition, which helps you decide what should and shouldn't alter your company's approach. Finally, reviewing your competitors' social profiles will assist you in ensuring that your marketing stands out and is distinctive to your brand.

How to Create a Social Media Marketing Strategy

Although social media continually evolves, most of the fundamental processes required for success remain constant. Essentially, you're doing the same procedures to develop a marketing strategy and narrow it down to a single channel.

Let's go over these procedures in further detail so you can start using them in your business.

Conduct Research on Your Buyer Personas and Target Audience

The first stage in developing a social media marketing plan is identifying your buyer personas and audience so that you can correctly target their requirements and interests.

Consider the people you want to reach, why, and how you would classify them as a group. For example, suppose your firm offers trendy leggings and joggers. In that case, you might categorize your target demographic as millennials who enjoy wearing stylish athletic clothes daily – a look known as athleisure.

You can evaluate what content will attract the type of followers and consumers you want by evaluating your buyer profiles and audience. Learn how to generate compelling content to keep your followers engaged as well.

Decide Which Social Media Channels You'll Use to Market

As a social media marketer, you must decide which channels to share your content. Regarding which social platforms your business should use, there isn't always a right or wrong answer - it's more about your target audience's demands and where they spend their time.

It is critical to know where your target audience is today and where they might be tomorrow. It is preferable to be ahead of the curve than behind it. For example, suppose you want to reach the target audience of athleisure-loving millennials. In that case, you should concentrate your social media efforts on Instagram, where millennials make up the majority of users.

Identify Your Most Essential Metrics and Key Performance Indicators (KPIs)

Your social media approach should be data-driven, regardless of your goals or industry. That involves concentrating on the social media analytics that are important. Rather than focusing on vanity metrics, investigate data that is directly related to your objectives.

What metrics are we discussing? Take a look at the breakdown below:

Reach. The number of unique users who saw your post is called post reach. How much of your material makes it into users' feeds?

Clicks. This is the number of people who have clicked on your content or account. Tracking clicks per campaign is critical for understanding what piques people's interest or pushes them to buy.

Engagement. The sum of all social interactions is divided by the total number of impressions. This reveals how well your audience perceives you and their readiness to communicate with you.

Hashtag presentation. What were your top hashtags? Which hashtags were most closely associated with your company? Having these answers can help influence the focus of your future content.

Organic and Paid Likes. These interactions are attributed to paid or organic content and a regular "Like" count. Given the difficulty of gaining organic engagement, many firms turn to advertising. Knowing these distinctions can help you budget your ad expenditure and the time you invest in various formats.

Sentiment. This metric measures how users react to your content, brand, or hashtag. Did your latest promotion offend customers? What kind of emotion is associated with your campaign hashtag? It's always a good idea to delve deeper and discover how people talk about or feel about your brand.

Research Your Competition

A competitive analysis lets you learn who your competitors are and what they do well (and poorly). You'll gain a clear feel of what's required in your business, which can help you define your own social media goals.

It will also help you in identifying opportunities. Perhaps one of your competitors is strong on Facebook but has made little effort on Twitter or Instagram. Rather than trying to entice followers away from a dominant player, you might prefer to concentrate your efforts on networks where your target audience is underserved.

Develop Original and Entertaining Content

With billions of social media users worldwide, there's no doubt that some of your followers — or individuals browsing your profile — have also seen your competitors or other businesses in your industry's material. This is why you need interesting social media content that sticks out and gives viewers a cause to click the "Follow" button and interact with your brand.

Not sure what constitutes interesting content?

First, conduct market research because what will be engaging relies on the audience. You may generate content that engages your audience's interests when you know what they like and need to know.

Consider the content your competitors share and how you may uniquely advertise your products. Also, use the functionality provided by the platform you're using. For example, you can use Facebook live broadcasts to convey the most recent information about a product launch or to hold a giveaway.

You can also solicit material from your present customers and advocates. You can accomplish this by re-posting their material or encouraging them to use a hashtag to share their own product experiences and photos.

Finally, take advantage of current trends. Social media trends are always changing, particularly on short-form video sites like TikTok. Don't be scared to participate, but be deliberate about how you do so. Identifying trends early on is the greatest way to profit without appearing inauthentic or desperate.

Establish a Posting Schedule

Using a social media management tool is one of the simplest methods to ensure your material gets spread as planned. You can use these tools to compose captions, prepare images and videos, and schedule posts in advance. They also share your material regularly and track your post interactions and engagement. Social media management software saves you time and allows you to concentrate on other duties.

There are several solutions possible; here are a few examples.

HubSpot

As part of its marketing platform, HubSpot provides a social media tool to help you produce and track your content and communicate with your followers. You may schedule and publish your content ahead of time and compare detailed information on your posts' engagement to evaluate better the performance of different platforms, content types, and publishing timings.

Sprout Social

Sprout Social is a social media marketing and management tool that will assist your team in organizing and planning content creation, managing campaigns, understanding engagement, and reviewing content reports and analysis.

Hootsuite

Hootsuite is a social media management software that allows you to search, schedule, manage, and report your content. You may schedule posts on your channels in advance and track your ROI with complete content analysis.

How Often Should You Post on Social Media?

As a general guideline, you should only post on social media when you have valuable stuff to contribute. That is, there is a reason why you are posting the stuff. This is how you'll strike the proper balance in frequently posting.

The most common error brands make in social media marketing is focusing on quantity rather than quality. They believe they must post daily, forcing themselves to write posts to fill up the calendar. The chances are that none of those posts will be beneficial to the ideal customer.

Posting two or three times per week with valuable material rather than seven times per week with only one or two quality pieces is preferable. There are numerous research and tools accessible to you that describe social media post frequency requirements by industry and platform. Every business is unique, so figure out what works best for your target demographic.

Then, you may start experimenting with more or fewer posts and other parameters like the time of day you publish on social media to see what gets the most engagement.

How to Evaluate the Impact and Results of Your Social Media Marketing

One of the most crucial components of social media marketing is ensuring that your efforts assist you in reaching your objectives. To figure this out, you'll need to keep track of your posts across all channels. This can be accomplished by reviewing and adjusting your social media stats.

Metrics for Social Media

Social media metrics are data about the success of your postings and your influence on your audience and customers across several platforms. These analytics may include information about your degree of engagement, likes, follows, shares, and all other interactions on each site.

Here are ten of the most critical metrics to monitor:

Engagement: Clicks, comments, likes, and reactions to your social media posts are examples of engagement. There are other platform-specific sorts of engagement, such as "Saved" Instagram posts and "Pinned" Pinterest posts.

Reach: This is the number of individuals who have seen any material related to your page or profile.

Followers: The amount of people who have clicked your "Follow" button on your profile and regularly view your stuff in their feeds.

Impressions: The number of times a post from your profile or page is viewed, regardless of whether your audience members click on it. This is common when someone scrolls through their newsfeed without clicking on anything.

Video views: The number of views a video receives on Facebook, Snapchat, Instagram, or any other social channel with video capability.

Profile visits: This is the number of people who have opened your social media page.

Mentions: The number of times your profile has been mentioned in posts by audience members.

Tags: When your audience adds the name of your company's profile or a hashtag to another post, this is referred to as tagging.

Reposts: When a member of your target audience shares a portion of your material on their profile.

Shares: These are posts your followers and audience copy and share with their networks.

By employing the same strategies used to create leads and drive conversions, you may affect all of these metrics, expand your social following, and improve overall engagement on your profile.

Also, note that the stats you focus on will differ depending on the season. Here's an example:

If you're just starting out, concentrate on growing your following and raising exposure. Reach, impressions and audience growth are the most important KPIs.

Focus on developing trust if you want to advance. Key indicators include likes, saves, comments, and direct messages.

If you're already established, concentrate on retaining and cultivating your customers. Key indicators include likes, saves, comments, and direct messages.

Focus on selling if you're introducing something. DMs and clickthrough rates are important stats.

Measuring Social Media Metrics

You can evaluate social media stats in various ways, including using the analytics tools integrated into your sites. Here are a couple of such examples:

- Twitter Analytics
- Facebook Analytics
- Instagram Insights

You might also use an analytics and tracking program like Google Analytics. This is a wonderful alternative if you want to track your social media and website stats. Finally, as previously discussed, many social media scheduling solutions include monitoring and tracking functions by default. These metrics tracking tools can help you discover what your followers and audience respond favorably to and what you should consider changing to increase engagement.

VIDEO AND VISUAL CONTENT CREATION

The act of generating topic ideas that appeal to your buyer persona, creating written or visual material around those ideas, and making that information available to your audience as a blog, video, infographic, or other content format is known as content creation.

What happens behind the scenes is content creation. This is how Google can provide the best solution to your problem. It's the YouTube videos you watch after a long day.

Content production is also how consumers learn about your company, brand, and products. This information assists you in attracting, engaging, and delighting prospects and customers. It attracts new users to your website and, as a result, produces cash for your firm.

Significance of Content Creation

The ultimate inbound marketing practice is content development. When you generate content, you give your audience free and helpful information, bring new customers to your website, and retain existing customers through quality engagement.

You're also adding significant value to your firm, as seen by the following content marketing statistics:

- Almost 40% of marketers consider content marketing to be a critical component of their marketing strategy. According to 81% of respondents, their company views content as a business strategy.

- According to research from B2B marketers, content marketing is an effective technique for nurturing leads (60%), generating income (51%), and establishing an audience of subscribers (47%).

- And 10% of marketers who blog report the greatest return on investment.

Content equals business expansion. So, let's start with the many sorts of content you can make and then go over your content strategy.

Blog Content Creation Ideas

Blog postings are one sort of content generation (the type you're currently consuming). Blogs may educate, entertain, and inspire their readers through the written word. When someone searches for something on Google, the results are frequently blog postings.

Blogging is time and effort well spent, and 56% of marketers think it is their most effective content approach. However, it can be difficult to concentrate your focus and begin writing. These are some tried-and-true blog content development options, in addition to opinion pieces and product announcement postings.

Respond to a Question

Start with questions from beginners if you're unsure which to answer first. These can serve as a basis for furthering the growth of your blog. Another technique to utilize questions as a starting point is to recall the queries you had as a novice. Even queries from your most recent experience can benefit others in your field.

Once you've determined the appropriate questions, create a comprehensive response. You may like to skip over the specifics, but this is where you can provide the most value to your audience.

People often hesitate to ask questions because they don't want to appear dumb. Anticipating and responding to their inquiries can assist you in gaining their trust. It can also help your search engine rankings.

Compare and Contrast Problem-Solving Approaches

Another way you can assist your readers is by assisting them in making a decision. There are answers available online, but it might often feel like there are too many. If you are an expert in your field, you may share your knowledge while also assisting buyers who want to make an informed purchase. When choosing what to compare, make sure the items have more similarities than differences.

For example, you wouldn't compare a project management tool to email marketing software. Be upfront and transparent when writing compare-and-contrast blogs for a product or service. Make a list of all the advantages and negatives you can think of. Then, explain in detail how you arrived at those conclusions.

Share Your Knowledge

Educational blogs are among the most popular. Consider a few things to consider if you want to use your blog as a teaching tool. When deciding on a topic, it's best to start simple. Instead of addressing a wide topic, pick a particular topic in which people in your sector may be interested.

Instead of writing about website design fundamentals, write about how to construct a car dealership's home page.

There are a few things to keep in mind as you begin creating how-to blogs:

- Create a clear framework with brief sentences and paragraphs. This will make it easy for people to understand your directions.

- If possible, avoid jargon and technical phrases and use examples to make new material easier to understand.

- Remember that your instructions should be simple enough for a beginner to understand, so don't skip steps or provide shortcuts.

- These pointers should assist your readers in learning while also increasing traffic and interest in your instructional content.

Series on a Daily, Monthly, or Weekly Basis

Writing a series of pieces can benefit your viewers and the growth of your site. A series will typically run for a predetermined amount of time. You can select to publish the series daily, weekly, or monthly. A series can produce content that can be easily used for different channels. For example, if you run a social media blog, you could adapt an Instagram Reels blog series into a podcast, ebook, or video.

This method makes it straightforward to investigate a specific issue thoroughly. It can help you position yourself as a thought leader and build internal and external ties.

Tests and Surveys

Blog surveys are an excellent method to gather feedback from your readers. This can assist with more than just website visitors.

Quiz and survey responses can also be useful to:

- Determine what other forms of content your audience enjoys.
- Select the products to promote and sell.
- Increase your social media following.
- Use interactive content to get viral.
- Prepare for customer service concerns.

Before you begin constructing a quiz or survey, identify your aims. Keeping your quizzes brief and adding incentives will help you get more responses.

Content Curation for Specific Audiences

While your blog may appeal to anyone, your ultimate goal is to connect with your ideal buyer personas. Curated content will make the most important individuals of your audience feel significant. This could imply that this audience becomes a community of promoters, sharing your information and encouraging others to purchase your products.

Considering this, it's a good idea to tailor material exclusively for this demographic. Assume you're in the business of selling sandals. You should provide separate information for folks who wear sandals all year and those who only wear sandals at particular seasons.

Begin your content curation with extensive buyer personas and competitor research. Next, design content clusters tailored specifically to that customer persona.

You'll also want to emphasize statements and insights from industry leaders in curated material. This content should not only inform a specific audience. It should give them the impression that they are a part of a select group.

Rejoice in Victories

The majority of blogs are evergreen. This means that once a blog is published online, it can be used as a resource for many years. As a result, blogs are an excellent location to celebrate victories. You may use your blog to celebrate, whether you're recognizing top-performing employees or thanking customers. Remember to rejoice in the simple things. Then, to make celebratory postings feel particularly special, use photographs, videos, and design.

Podcast Content Creation Ideas

Listening to podcasts is similar to listening to the radio. However, anyone can create and broadcast a podcast. This means that both experienced and inexperienced podcast hosts are fighting for the same amount of listening time.

However, they have a large audience, with 28% of Americans aged 12 and above listening to podcasts weekly. When the audience likes the host and wants to learn something from them, podcasts become even more compelling. Continue reading for more podcast content production suggestions.

A great podcast usually starts with a wonderful idea and then expands on it with the audience's and expert's responses. Educational podcasts and storytelling podcasts are both popular. If this is your first podcast, make sure to post regularly. Sticking to the same format for each episode is also a good idea. Aside from that, it's all about being your true self.

Thought Direction

This form of podcast content focuses on your professional background. Include case studies and other real-world events in this subject. Remember that your audience is tuning in for various reasons and often has varying levels of industry experience. So, provide insights for various listeners and present advice you believe your listeners could use.

Conduct Influencer Interviews

Knowing who to interview is the first step in adding influencer interviews to your podcast. Don't limit yourself to the greatest stars. Instead, select engaging people who can value your listeners' lives. Make an effort to investigate your guests and ask unique questions. For example, the success of the YouTube show "Hot Ones" can be partly attributed to the well-researched questions that its host asks each celebrity guest.

Other strategies for making the most of influencer interviews on your podcast include:

- Requesting suggestions from followers
- Encourage your featured influencer's followers to participate.

Discuss Current Trends

Trends make excellent podcast fodder. Whether you're talking about a long-term trend or the latest fad, this is an excellent backdrop for demonstrating how your items are related to what's new. While many people listen to daily or weekly news podcasts, most podcasts, like blogs, are evergreen. Many podcast listeners will tune in years after the show's initial publication. This implies that you should connect trends to larger issues.

Contests & Prizes

Contests allow your podcast listeners to participate in a fun way while also offering you the opportunity to build your subscriber base. Posting about a prize or giveaway on social media is one approach to starting a podcast contest. Another possibility is to hold interactive contests in which listeners can call in to be a part of the podcast. If you intend to offer a prize, make it distinctive and appropriate for your target audience.

Video Content Creation Ideas

Whether you want to share videos on social media or on YouTube, video marketing is a content generation that is becoming increasingly popular. Both short-form and long-form videos have a role in your content strategy. So, make sure to think of ideas for both forms of content.

According to 86% of video marketers, video generates leads successfully. As a result, original video marketing is vital for anyone involved in content creation.

Behind-the-scenes or time-lapse videos are examples of good video content ideas. Let's go through some more excellent video content development ideas.

Animate Difficult-to-Understand Concepts

Animation aids in the comprehension of new or complex information. So, use video to demonstrate your product's work or to discuss the unique problem it answers. Choose circumstances to which people can relate that are obviously related to your product. Whether you utilize computer animation or stop-motion animation, animation can bring a dull subject to life.

For example, tech solutions frequently tackle problems the common user does not encounter daily, such as a broken connection with an API. But how about an animation of what occurs when your home's wireless goes out? A film using this situation could help the typical user understand that abstract concept.

Adapt Blog Content

Another simple video concept is to use your most popular blog's text as a voiceover. Long blogs create excellent video series content. You can also turn essential blog themes into bite-sized videos for social media posts. Then, include your videos in your blog postings. This provides individuals who find your site through search engines with another option for finding the content they seek.

Tutorials and How-Tos

In video formats, how-to content is also quite popular. Stick to brief and specific stages when creating a compelling instructional film. You don't want to leave anything out, but you also don't want to overload your audience with information. Use basic visual phases to assist your visitors in learning, and end with a clear call to action.

Participating in the comments section of these videos is also a good idea. This reassures your audience that you are available if they have any further inquiries and may inspire you to create more video ideas.

Product Demonstrations and Novel Use Cases

Product demos can let potential clients see how they can use your items. It's also an opportunity for you to discuss some of your product design processes. You can develop a relationship with your viewers by explaining the problem you initially solved with your product and how the answer altered during the process. This relationship fosters trust and increases their likelihood of engaging with you and your offerings.

Unusually show your product's functionality. For example, Blendtec's "Will It Blend?" video series on YouTube was a hit because it demonstrated more than simply the capability of its blender. They were creative in that they solicited user feedback for each film. The movies involved blending materials that you wouldn't ordinarily put in a blender, such as cell phones, golf balls, and glow sticks.

You can also customize the video material. Video product demos are an excellent way to introduce specific customers to your items.

Ideas for Image-Based Content

You might want to use creative visuals in your blog or social media posts. Infographics, photographs, GIFs, memes, sketches, or screenshots are acceptable. This form of content development normally necessitates the assistance of a graphic designer or a design tool. Businesses use photo and image-based posts the most to improve audience engagement.

As you develop visual material, ensure you understand the fundamentals. These are some examples:

- Choose the best topic to show your point.
- Consider composition.

- Make use of contrast and color.
- Maintain simplicity.

Storytelling in Pictures

Visual material is ideal for telling stories quickly. Remember to show, not tell, when you begin to explore with storytelling. Assume you're sharing a narrative about achieving a difficult sales objective. A photo of a salesperson on the phone does not tell the same story as a picture of that same salesperson scaling a huge mountain. Try to emphasize the action and drama of each scene in your photographs by using setting, dress, lighting, and motion.

User-Generated Content (UGC)

Fans of your products are frequently looking for opportunities to participate. And nothing beats user-generated content to demonstrate to your fans that you value their feedback. To encourage your users to create and share content for your brand, invite them to participate. To begin, try a custom hashtag or a social media contest. Email is also an excellent way to collect your consumers' photos, quotations, and tales.

However, do not use user-generated content without their permission. You should also be sure to give users credit for their work. Nothing can harm your connection with customers more than exploiting their photographs without their permission.

Information Graphics

Evidence shows that data visualization can reduce errors and enhance learning and retention by up to 80%. If you wish to integrate infographics into your content production plan, keep the following best practices in mind:

- Select the appropriate facts for your intended audience.
- Select the best graph or chart for your data.
- Conduct your research
- Create a simple visual tale.
- Don't include too much information.
- Make your essential points simple to read and recall.

Take a Look Behind the Scenes

It is fascinating for your readers to learn about industry and product secrets. It's also an interesting approach to offer information on how your products are made, packaged, and updated. Begin with a plan to produce graphics transporting your viewers behind the scenes. Make it cool whether you're sharing images from a tour of your manufacturing facility or capturing a typical day on social media.

Consider lighting, composition, and minor elements. A big dirty garbage can or a caution sign in the background will mar a beautiful product image. Simultaneously, make your photographs feel genuine. Set up your images in a setting that appears too flawless to be true.

CONTENT PERSONALIZATION AND SEGMENTATION

All brands struggle to develop meaningful interactions and messages with their customer base. Understanding the differences and similarities between data, personalization, and segmentation is required to achieve that goal. Up to 93% of internet users say commercial communications aren't relevant to them, and 90% say irrelevant material irritates them. Consumers want brands to understand what's going on in their life. However, this won't be easy if businesses do not understand and embrace the differences between segmentation and customization.

Companies and marketers frequently use personalization, segmentation, and targeting interchangeably. They all have the same purpose in mind: to create content that reflects what the reader, viewer, or listener desires. However, each strategy takes a distinct approach. When marketers discuss goals, methods, and execution, everyone must speak the same language.

Consider it this way:

Disney, for example, divides its TV audience into groups based on mutual interests. The Disney Channel's audience is distinct from that of ESPN. Streaming services like Netflix tailor their programming by recommending new episodes based on what they know about a person's or household's viewing habits. Hence, personalization, segmentation, or both may be used in your content marketing program at different periods for different reasons.

How Do Segmentation and Personalization Differ?

Companies and marketers frequently use personalization, segmentation, and targeting interchangeably. The reality is that each of these tactics is unique and has different connotations. When marketers discuss goals, methods, and execution, everyone must speak the same language.

Segmentation: It's About the Marketer

Segmentation is a critical element in effective marketing. Some marketers refer to this as segmentation targeting. It entails discovering similar groups of potential clients based on pertinent information that marketers can utilize to deliver a combination of techniques to achieve extraordinary outcomes.

Segmentation often follows a set of descriptors, including demographic or psychographic factors from a possible client base. Customer segments include the following:

- **Behavioral segmentation**: Data about a customer's actions (or inactions), average order value, browsing history, consuming (or spending) patterns, feature use, session frequency, and other factors are included in behavioral segmentation.

- **Demographic segmentation**: This contains a customer's age, gender, income, marital status, occupation, and other information.

- **Geographic segmentation**: This might include both local and wide geographic data. Local information refers to individual towns or counties. Broad data is information about a customer's city, state, or country of residence.

- **Psychographic segmentation:** This is where marketers acquire information on their customers' attitudes, interests, personality traits, values, and other characteristics.

- **Technographic segmentation:** Marketers collect information about a customer's preferred mobile devices, software, and technology, among other things.

When Should You Use Segmentation?

Marketers should use segmentation early in the campaign's life cycle. As marketers collect and apply data, they better understand their target audience. They can then tailor their messaging to the customer's difficulties, needs, and desires.

A marketer's data is useless unless they can make a story or build a message about their clients. Who are the clients? What are their expectations from the brand's products or services? Can you recognize their difficulties? Marketers can use their acquired data to construct a narrative that effectively communicates marketing strategies to customers and team members.

Marketers can utilize segmentation in marketing tactics after they have enough data to develop a narrative for each part of their client base. This enables marketers to build manageable web presences to construct and customize content.

Personalization: It's about the Customer

Personalization entails locating a specific client within a group. For instance, we might have a customer named John in the golfing area. John is a beginner with countless enjoyable experiences with his beginner golf club set with his closest buddies. This could include scheduling time at a driving range or visiting golf courses.

Personalization is about how a company may alleviate that person's pain point or need. Understanding the customer's goal and delivering customized experiences around that intent is required.

- Is the customer just beginning their adventure (e.g., shopping) and looking for ideas?
- Are they prepared to make a decision and look for the best deal?
- Is the consumer already aware of what they want and concerned about the purchase?

When Should You Use Personalization?

Each time a customer interacts with a brand, their intent can shift. Their intent can also shift during a single contact. Marketers must, therefore, grasp the customer's demands beyond categorization. Identifying a customer's intent entails marketers employing rules-based logic to analyze numerous data points.

- How did the buyer discover our website?
- Which email messages do they respond to?
- What is their current geolocation?
- What are they looking for specifically, and which sites do they interact with the most?
- When and how frequently do they carry out these actions?

Personalization should occur whenever people contact a company, regardless of the content or medium. For example, on a brand's website, this may imply displaying product recommendations based on customer requirements. If the brand employs a chatbot, it may be able to provide better support after recognizing the customer's account. This could imply employing a mobile app to notify customers about a promotion or sale in a physical store.

Tips to Help You Personalize Your Content and Segment Your Audiences

Segment During Planning, Personalize for Delivery

Collect segmentation data to help plan content calendar, restrict target, and understand the complexity of your audience. Personalization requires delivering contextually relevant content based on segmentation and other data.

Personalization will fail if you do not grasp audience segmentation. Netflix, for example, utilizes machine learning algorithms to segment its client bases, then personalizes content distribution by providing recommended content based on the assumption that if you liked X, you'll definitely like Y. The system believes you'll like Y because others in your demographic also liked X and loved Y.

Use Rules and Tagging to Avoid Manual Overload

Segmentation occurs while creating marketing assets, such as the go-to-market strategy, multiple channels of distribution, and, eventually, the destinations or experiences to which the audience will be directed. The personalization part is where that comes to life for the buyer. When this occurs, you can provide personalization in methods ranging from knowing their first name to delivering the material someone is looking for at that precise moment.

It's challenging to imagine individually tailoring for every buyer one at a time. That is why you require segmentation rules. When you can apply those via content tags, you may consider matching everything together.

Invest in Infrastructure to Allow for Scalable Content Reuse for Efficient Personalization

The need for more material to satisfy the ever-increasing need for a customer's attention is the same difficulty that personalizing content and scaling content marketing face. The solution is to repurpose content.

To successfully and efficiently reuse material, you must:

- Long-form content should be broken down into compact, agile, reusable, format-free components.
- Create new content by combining small, agile, reusable, format-free components.
- Create components for reuse utilizing the best standards for authoring.
- Organize and tag your stuff so that it is easily accessible.
- Create as many information assets as you need by combining and recombining your components.
- Format your information assets at the point of publication.

You will also want an architecture that allows for component-based authoring and single-sourcing. Reusing the same material for new and different deliverables saves time and money and allows you to customize and scale content.

Employees Are Excellent Personalizers

Personalization entails sending marketing communications from other real individuals to real people. Personalization is not some automatic method to appear to care about your prospects. That is why we feel that employee activation is the future marketing strategy. Encourage your employees to participate in social media by creating content, sharing what they know, and connecting with actual people. That is the only method to develop personalization that effectively attracts top staff and new customers to your company.

Segment to Resonate - And Track the Results

According to a recent Contently study, only 56% of marketers developed tailored content with specific consumer profiles in mind. This figure is very low. To break through, you must create content with a specific persona in mind.

You must be intimately familiar with your target audience. Discuss their problems, needs, and opportunities. Furthermore, you should preferably use a content marketing platform to classify each piece of content by persona, assess how well your content performs against each target group, and optimize your program accordingly.

ABM Success Requires Personalization

An account-based marketing program can benefit greatly from a hyper-personalized strategy. Individuals should feel they are obtaining all the answers they require, almost as if they have a personal shopper. They should have the impression that you are with them throughout their journey.

On the other hand, companies must be cautious of going down the dark, gloomy route. It's not about proving to them that you know who they are if they're on your site and you've never spoken to them before. It is all about listening to, using the proper signals, and providing tailored value.

Go for Dynamic Personalization, but Keep It Simple

When personalization and segmentation are dynamic and responsive to the consumer journey, they both shine. Some static segmentation is beneficial, such as developing and distributing information based on personas (particularly if personas are solid and up to date). However, real-time personalization based on customer behavior will be even more effective in the long run because it is timely, personalized, and hyper-relevant to what the user is looking for at the time.

The tendency to become overly complex is a possible shortcoming of personalization and segmentation. With apparently infinite ways to slice and dice audience data, content marketing projects can become hyper-personalized, making it difficult to determine which personalization is most beneficial. It's advisable to start simple and focus on the most critical one or two criteria.

You Need Both

The biggest mistake in personalization and segmentation is not implementing either method. If brands are not focused on customizing or segmenting audiences (and increasing such efforts), they are missing out on critical customer data and optimization.

The usefulness of segmentation is that it groups clients based on comparable identifiable qualities, such as demographic information or similar digital activity habits. Brands can make recommendations for "customers like you" while also assisting in improving marketing campaign performance. Brands can learn more about their audiences through segmentation, allowing them to customize their communications and outreach to meet the demands of their customers better.

Personalization adds value by ensuring customers receive the most optimized and relevant experiences and messaging for their specific needs.

Personalization provides the appropriate information for a customer's particular journey with a brand and can help guarantee their queries are answered. Personalization also aids conversions, client retention, and the development of trust between customers and brands.

Creating Better Marketing Strategies Using Segmentation and Personalization

When customers visit websites, they demand individualized experiences. Some people may be hesitant or unwilling to disclose information for these customized experiences to be created. However, this does not change their level of expectation. Marketers can quickly overcome this difficulty by tracking customers' click tendencies. Tracking this information allows brands and marketers to establish what is important to this person and, as a result, deliver a more tailored experience.

Regarding email messages, marketers can gauge customers' interest based on how they respond to specific messages. For example, a website may provide a free booklet, tutorial, or discount coupon in exchange for users' names and email addresses. This reply indicates to marketers that the person is interested in the messaging. As a result, they can personalize future messages and present more web assets based on that interest.

By combining segmentation and personalization, marketers can meet their customers where they are. These tactics are especially effective in today's digital and hybrid retail contexts. This is because marketers can pique a customer's interest by appealing to them individually. Segmentation enables marketers to develop content for certain customer groups, whereas personalization entails delving deeper into each client within a segment individually. Both of these tactics have their time and place. Combining them increases the efficacy of any brand's marketing plan.

CONTENT DISTRIBUTION AND PROMOTION

F or good reason, content promotion and distribution have been hot themes in growth marketing. Brands that have struggled to achieve success through content marketing initiatives are realizing that they require more than just a favorite social media outlet. A failing content distribution strategy is frequently the result of an audience problem rather than a problem with the content or the platform.

Even the best blog post, social network post, paid channel, or other content might not naturally reach a target demographic. In these circumstances, an expert content marketer understands that focused promotion methods must be in place for campaigns to work and reach an audience. But, despite all the talk about the importance of promotion and distribution, the two terms are still used arbitrarily, muddying the content marketing waters. It is time for some explanation.

The Evolution of Content Distribution

The content promotion sector has grown significantly since 2013, and semantics have evolved. Email marketing, social media marketing, influencer marketing, and other methods for content dissemination have all evolved at a rapid pace. Consumers have chugged along to catch up, whether it's through a Facebook group, Google Ads, a social media platform, or another distribution route.

Most importantly, content distribution has emerged as the online marketplace's favorite keyword. Most big companies and media sources increasingly focus on a revamped distribution strategy to increase brand recognition.

However, some aspects of developing a content distribution strategy have remained hazy. What is the difference between content distribution and content promotion?

The Umbrella of Content Promotion

Jordan Kasteler described a three-pronged approach to content promotion in August of 2013. This description is consistent with Forrester's classification of marketing media types: owned, paid, and earned.

As Kasteler pointed out, we can separate content promotion into three categories. Each component of your content distribution strategy is synonymous with marketing strategy jargon you've probably heard before broadcasting, distribution, and digital PR.

So, to answer the issue on which this post is based, distribution is just the commercial arm of content promotion.

Broadcasting

Broadcasting is the act of distributing content from its original source via owned channels controlled by a brand. Most brands are familiar with and use this form of content promotion regularly, generally through social media or another regulated channel.

Most of the time, the audience watching the promoted material is already familiar with the brand and the default content type. This is because they have opted into those digital marketing platforms. The following are some examples of promoting your content or using broadcasting as a distribution channel.

- **Social Media Posts:** A brand's content is shared on social media platforms such as Facebook, Twitter, Instagram, LinkedIn, Pinterest, and YouTube.

- **RSS Feeds:** A brand provides existing information to those who have requested to get it regularly.

- **Email:** A brand's content is disseminated through tailored emails to contacts who have voluntarily opted into previous interactions with that brand.

Distribution

The process of paying to leverage media channels to reach new consumers with content offerings is known as distribution. A brand does not own the channels via which it promotes its content in the event of paid content distribution. As a result, a brand rents channels for its content kinds by paying to access them for a limited time or amount of clicks.

Many brands are beginning to embrace this concept of content distribution, with some achieving exceptional success. The strategies listed below are examples of paid content promotion or distribution.

- **Sponsored Articles**: A form of advertising in the form of editorial material authored in-house or by the publisher and published in a media source. Video content is also effective these days.

- **Press Releases**: A formal statement issued by a brand to media outlets.

- **Sponsored Social Updates**: A sponsored post that appears in the news feed of a social media outlet. These advertisements typically target a new audience.

- **Sponsored Recommendations**: A Content Amplification Network adds native, sponsored call-to-actions to current content. Consider Outbrain or Taboola.

- **Native Newsletter**: Sponsored content within an independent third-party email newsletter is referred to as a native newsletter.

Digital PR

The technique of using outreach attempts to persuade a third party is known as digital PR. It doesn't matter if it's a target audience member, a social media personality, a publisher, or an influencer. Anyone can interact with information and share it on their own social media networks.

The purpose of digital PR, like that of content distribution, is to reach a new audience with a content offer. According to a Nielsen research, earned media is the most trusted source of information worldwide.

Most earned media returns can only be realized through trustworthy partnerships that have been established over time by demonstrating credibility and consistency through dependable content distribution methods. Valuable material is undoubtedly beneficial to the process. The following are some examples of earned media outcomes via digital PR.

- **News coverage**: unbiased reporting on a brand's content by a well-known media source channel.

- **Editorial Coverage**: A media outlet channel's independent reporting on a brand's content.

- **Influencer Advocacy:** A brand's content is promoted by an industry influencer via their channel or other networks.

- **Bylined Column**: A consistent, ongoing publishing opportunity on a reputable channel or media site.

- **Bylined Article**: A one-time or unscheduled individual contribution to a third-party publication.

- **Content syndication**: This is republishing a brand's content on another website or marketing channel.

Combine Earned, Owned, and Paid Promotion to Maximize Results

The days of issuing a press release and then calling it a day are over. Social media has grown, providing marketers with numerous platforms for content dissemination. Any brand awareness message must find its way onto a content distribution channel corresponding to the target audience's preferences. Content promotion aims to get material in front of the right people. It's as simple as that.

It is pointless if your target audience cannot find your material. It's inefficient and a waste of time. In many circumstances, promotion is required to achieve noticeable outcomes. Content marketers can no longer avoid advertising. There is no guarantee that any audience will discover exceptional content independently.

Like most other goal-oriented marketing methods, content promotion has more than one way to skin a cat. Earned, owned, and paid promotions are all viable methods of content marketing distribution in their own right. However, as Kasteler points out in his approach to content promotion, a unified content distribution platform plan that employs all three would provide the most visibility, traffic, and engagement.

Multichannel Distribution Strategy: Amplifying Reach and Visibility

A multichannel distribution strategy is key to maximizing your reach and visibility in digital marketing. It involves using multiple online platforms and channels to distribute your content and engage with your target audience. This strategy allows you to meet your audience where they are, diversify your marketing efforts, and create a cohesive online presence. Here's how to make the most of a multichannel distribution strategy:

Identify Your Target Channels: Start by identifying the most relevant online channels for your audience and industry. Common channels include social media platforms (e.g., Facebook, Instagram, Twitter, LinkedIn), email marketing, content marketing (e.g., blogs, podcasts, videos), paid advertising (e.g., Google Ads, Facebook Ads), and SEO (search engine optimization).

Tailor Content to Each Channel: Each channel has its own unique audience, format, and communication style. Adapt your content to fit the characteristics of each platform. For example, short and visually appealing content may work well on Instagram, while longer-form content and professional insights are better suited for LinkedIn.

Maintain Brand Consistency: While tailoring content, ensure that your brand voice, messaging, and visual identity remain consistent across all channels. This consistency helps build brand recognition and trust.

Use Cross-Promotion: Promote your content across different channels to cross-pollinate your audience. For example, share your blog posts on social media, promote your social media accounts in your emails, and include links to your YouTube videos on your website.

Leverage Automation: Automation tools can help streamline your multichannel distribution efforts. Use email marketing automation, social media scheduling tools, and content management systems to ensure consistent and timely distribution.

Engage Actively: Don't just publish and forget. Engage actively with your audience on each channel. Respond to comments, answer questions, and participate in discussions. Engagement enhances your brand's credibility and fosters a sense of community.

Measure and Analyze: Use analytics tools to track the performance of your content on each channel. Monitor metrics like engagement rates, click-through rates, conversion rates, and audience demographics. Adjust your strategy based on the insights you gather.

Test and Optimize: Continually test different types of content, posting schedules, and distribution channels to determine what works best for your audience. Optimization is an ongoing process.

Consider Paid Advertising: Incorporate paid advertising into your multichannel strategy to amplify your reach. Paid ads can target specific demographics and interests, ensuring your content reaches the right audience.

Stay Updated: Digital marketing is constantly evolving. Stay updated on industry trends, algorithm changes, and emerging channels to adapt your strategy accordingly.

A well-executed multichannel distribution strategy can significantly expand your brand's reach and visibility in the digital landscape. By tailoring your content, maintaining consistency, actively engaging with your audience, and utilizing the right tools, you can effectively connect with your target audience across various online channels, driving engagement and achieving your marketing goals.

Maximizing Organic Reach: Social Sharing, SEO, and Email Marketing

In digital marketing, organic reach is the holy grail. It's connecting with your audience without relying solely on paid advertising. To maximize organic reach, you need a strategic approach encompassing social sharing, search engine optimization (SEO), and email marketing. Here's how to make the most of each:

Social Sharing

- **Create Shareable Content:** Craft content that resonates with your audience and provides value. Content that entertains, educates or inspires is more likely to be shared.

- **Engage and Interact:** Actively engage with your audience on social media platforms. Respond to comments, answer questions and foster discussions. This engagement encourages users to share your content.

- **Leverage User-Generated Content:** Encourage your audience to create and share content related to your brand. User-generated content serves as authentic testimonials and can be highly shareable.

- **Use Visuals:** Visual content, such as images, videos, and infographics, tends to be more shareable than plain text. Invest in compelling visuals that convey your message effectively.

- **Leverage Hashtags:** Use relevant and trending hashtags to increase the discoverability of your posts. Hashtags expand your content's reach beyond your immediate followers.

SEO (Search Engine Optimization)

- **Keyword Research:** Identify relevant keywords and phrases your audience is searching for. Use tools like Google Keyword Planner, SEMrush, or Ahrefs to find valuable keywords.

- **On-Page Optimization:** Optimize your website content for search engines by including keywords in titles, headings, and meta descriptions. Use schema markup to enhance search result visibility.

- **High-Quality Content:** Create informative, well-structured, and valuable content for your audience. High-quality content is more likely to rank well in search results.

- **Link Building:** Build a network of high-quality backlinks to your content. Quality links from authoritative sources can boost your search engine rankings.

- **Mobile Optimization:** Ensure your website is mobile-friendly, as search engines favor mobile-responsive websites.

- **Local SEO:** If you have a local business, optimize your website for local search by creating a Google My Business listing and acquiring local backlinks.

Email Marketing

- **Segmentation:** Segment your email list based on audience demographics, behavior, and preferences. Send targeted content that is relevant to each segment.

- **Personalization:** Personalize your email content, including subject lines and recommendations. Personalized emails tend to have higher open and click-through rates.

- **A/B Testing:** Continuously test different elements of your email campaigns, such as subject lines, content, and send times, to optimize performance.

- **Engagement:** Encourage engagement with your emails by including interactive elements like polls, surveys, and product recommendations.

- **Consistency:** Maintain a consistent email marketing schedule to keep your audience engaged and informed.

- **Monitor Analytics:** Use email marketing analytics to track open rates, click-through rates, conversion rates, and other key metrics. Analyze the data to refine your email campaigns.

- **Opt-In and Unsubscribe Options:** Ensure subscribers can easily opt in and unsubscribe from their emails. This fosters trust and compliance with email regulations.

Maximizing organic reach requires a multifaceted approach that combines the power of social sharing, SEO, and email marketing. By creating shareable content, optimizing for search engines, and delivering personalized emails, you can connect with your audience meaningfully while expanding your brand's visibility organically.

BUILDING RELATIONSHIPS AND AUTHORITY

Building trust with your audience is important to any content marketing plan. When you develop trust, you also build authority. When you check those two boxes, you create connections that lead to long-term, mutually beneficial relationships.

Links from peers, followers, customers, and admirers are examples of "mutually beneficial" content. It's that simple: if you provide genuine value, they will repay you in kind. The difficulty is, how do you even begin to develop trust and connections? What should you do right away?

Content as Thought Leadership: Establishing Your Brand as an Industry Expert

In the competitive digital marketing landscape, positioning your brand as a thought leader within your industry is a strategic advantage. Thought leadership builds trust with your audience and sets you apart from competitors. Here's how to use content to establish your brand as an industry expert:

In-Depth, Insightful Content: Produce high-quality, in-depth content that provides valuable insights and solutions to industry-specific challenges. This could include whitepapers, research reports, long-form articles, and case studies. Thought leadership content should demonstrate a deep understanding of your field and offer unique perspectives.

Address Industry Trends and Challenges: Stay ahead of industry trends and address challenges that your audience faces. Offering solutions and guidance on current issues positions your brand as a valuable resource.

Consistency and Frequency: Consistency is key to thought leadership. Regularly publish content on your website, blog, or relevant industry publications. Consistent publishing establishes your brand's authority over time.

Expert Opinions and Interviews: Leverage the expertise of your team members. Feature interviews, opinion pieces, or guest posts from your executives and subject matter experts. Highlight their knowledge and experiences to reinforce your brand's credibility.

Original Research and Data: Conduct original research within your industry and publish the results. Data-driven insights are valuable and can make your brand a go-to source for industry information.

Engage in Industry Conversations: Participate in industry events, webinars, and conferences. Share your knowledge and engage in discussions. Live interactions can establish your brand as a thought leader in real time.

Thoughtful Content Curation: Curate content from other experts in your field and provide your own commentary and insights. This demonstrates that you are well-versed in industry developments and are actively engaging with industry thought leaders.

Educational Resources: Create educational resources, such as ebooks, how-to guides, and video tutorials, that help your audience solve problems and gain a deeper understanding of industry topics.

User-Generated Content: Encourage your audience to share their success stories and experiences with your products or services. Showcase user-generated content to demonstrate real-world applications and results.

Networking and Collaboration: Build relationships with other industry leaders and influencers. Collaborate on content, joint webinars, or co-authored articles. Associating your brand with respected experts enhances your credibility.

Social Media Engagement: Engage in conversations on social media platforms related to your industry. Share your thoughts, insights, and content to showcase your expertise.

Measure and Adjust: Regularly analyze the performance of your thought leadership content. Track website traffic, engagement rates, social shares, and lead generation metrics. Use these insights to refine your strategy.

Be Authentic: Authenticity is crucial for thought leadership. Be transparent, honest, and genuine in your communications. Authenticity builds trust and credibility.

Establishing your brand as an industry expert through thought leadership content is a long-term endeavor. It requires dedication, consistent effort, and a genuine commitment to delivering value to your audience. Over time, your brand will become synonymous with expertise and leadership in your field, fostering trust and loyalty among your customers and peers.

Content Collaborations: Guest Posts, Interviews, and Cross-Promotion

In the ever-evolving digital marketing landscape, content collaborations have emerged as a potent strategy for expanding one's reach, enhancing credibility, and fostering mutually beneficial relationships within the industry. This essay explores three key forms of content collaborations: guest posts, interviews, and cross-promotion, highlighting their significance and how they contribute to the success of brands and individuals in the digital sphere.

Guest Posts

Guest posting, also known as guest blogging, involves creating content for publication on someone else's website or blog. This collaborative approach offers several advantages for both the host and the guest contributor.

For the host, guest posts provide fresh perspectives and diverse content, which can be especially valuable when the guest is an industry expert or thought leader. It enriches the host's content portfolio, attracting a wider audience and improving search engine rankings through backlinks. Guest posts also introduce the host's audience to new voices and ideas, increasing engagement and credibility.

For the guest contributor, writing guest posts provides an opportunity to showcase expertise, reach a broader audience, and build backlinks to their own website or blog. By aligning with respected hosts, guest contributors can leverage the host's established credibility to enhance their own reputation as industry experts.

Interviews

Interviews are a powerful content collaboration tool that allows two parties to engage in a dynamic conversation, often with one acting as the interviewer and the other as the interviewee. Interviews can take various forms, including written, audio, or video formats.

Interviews offer numerous benefits for both parties. They provide fresh and engaging content that captivates the audience's attention. The interviewer benefits from the interviewee's insights and knowledge, elevating the quality of the content. Meanwhile, the interviewee gains exposure to the host's audience, building credibility and authority within the industry.

Moreover, interviews foster a sense of community and collaboration within the industry. They encourage open dialogue and knowledge-sharing, making them valuable in cultivating relationships with peers, competitors, and potential collaborators.

Cross-Promotion

Cross-promotion involves two or more parties promoting each other's content, products, or services to their respective audiences. This collaboration strategy is highly effective in broadening reach and gaining access to a partner's audience.

Cross-promotion is particularly beneficial on social media platforms, where brands and individuals can share each other's content, tag one another, or even co-host events or giveaways. This strategy leverages the power of social proof and endorsement, as audiences tend to trust recommendations from sources they already follow.

Additionally, cross-promotion enables brands to tap into complementary audiences. For example, a fashion brand collaborating with a makeup artist can reach customers interested in both fashion and beauty. This synergy boosts engagement and can lead to new followers, customers, or subscribers.

Therefore, content collaborations, including guest posts, interviews, and cross-promotion, are invaluable tools in the digital marketing toolkit. They facilitate knowledge sharing, expand reach, enhance credibility, and foster beneficial relationships within the industry. In an era where collaboration and authenticity are highly valued, these strategies benefit individual brands and contribute to a thriving and interconnected digital ecosystem. Embracing these collaboration opportunities can elevate one's presence and impact in the ever-evolving world of digital marketing.

Earning Backlinks: Boosting SEO and Credibility through High-Quality Content

Search engine optimization (SEO) remains a pivotal factor in determining the online success of businesses and websites. Among the many components of SEO, backlinks hold a distinct significance. They contribute to improving search engine rankings and add a layer of credibility to a website. This essay delves into the art of earning backlinks by creating high-quality content and elucidates its dual impact on SEO enhancement and bolstering credibility.

The Significance of Backlinks

Backlinks, also known as inbound or incoming links, are hyperlinks from one website to another. They serve as a testament to the authority and relevance of a webpage. Search engines, particularly Google, consider backlinks as a vote of confidence from one site to another. The more reputable and authoritative websites that link to a particular page, the more credible and valuable that page appears in the eyes of search engines.

High-Quality Content as a Backlink Magnet

One of the most effective and ethical ways to earn backlinks is by creating and disseminating high-quality content. High-quality content is content that is not only informative and relevant but also resonates with the target audience. When content is well-researched, well-written, and offers value, it becomes inherently link-worthy. Here's how high-quality content can attract backlinks:

- **Valuable Resources:** Authoritative and well-informed content, such as comprehensive guides, research studies, and informative articles, becomes a valuable resource for others in the same niche. Website owners and bloggers are more likely to link to such content to provide their readers with valuable information.

- **Natural Link Attraction:** When content is genuinely valuable, other websites are more inclined to link to it naturally. These natural, organic backlinks are highly coveted in the SEO world as they are seen as genuine endorsements of a website's credibility and expertise.

- **Social Sharing:** High-quality content tends to get shared on social media platforms and within industry communities. This increased visibility often leads to more websites discovering and linking to the content.

- **Guest Posting:** Guest posting on reputable websites in your niche allows you to showcase your expertise through valuable content while earning backlinks to your own site. This mutual benefit encourages collaboration and link-building.

The SEO Benefits of Backlinks

While backlinks offer many advantages, their primary role in SEO cannot be overstated. Here's how backlinks enhance SEO:

- **Improved Search Engine Rankings:** Search engines like Google use backlinks as a major ranking factor. Websites with a strong backlink profile tend to rank higher in search results, leading to increased organic traffic.

- **Enhanced Crawling and Indexing:** Search engine bots use backlinks to discover and index new web pages. A robust backlink profile ensures that your content is crawled and indexed promptly.

- **Keyword Relevance:** Backlinks from websites with content related to yours provide context and relevance to search engines. This helps search engines understand your content, enhancing keyword rankings.

Credibility and Trust

Beyond the SEO advantages, backlinks contribute significantly to a website's credibility and trustworthiness. When other reputable websites link to yours, it's akin to a vote of confidence in your expertise and content quality. Users and potential customers are more likely to trust and engage with a website that boasts credible backlinks from authoritative sources. This credibility extends to your brand and can increase conversions and customer loyalty.

So, earning backlinks through creating high-quality content is a multifaceted strategy that intertwines the realms of SEO enhancement and the bolstering of credibility. High-quality content attracts backlinks naturally, helps websites climb search engine rankings, and builds user trust. In the dynamic world of digital marketing, the symbiotic relationship between high-quality content and backlinks remains a cornerstone of online success, enabling websites to thrive in the ever-competitive digital landscape.

NAVIGATING CHALLENGES AND TRENDS

The marketing scene is considerably becoming more competitive and unpredictable. It is increasingly crucial for marketers to keep ahead of the curve to be successful. As a result, marketers must work hard to grasp the trends and devise a solid strategy tailored to their target demographic.

Begin by examining your existing consumer base and their actions. Knowing who your consumers are isn't enough; you also need to understand how they interact with your company both online and offline. With this information, you can build bespoke messaging suited to each customer segment, which will help you stand out from the competition.

Invest in market research to gain new insights into prospective possibilities and dangers within and beyond the sector. Finally, keep up with developing technology and ensure that all advertising is mobile device optimized.

Faster loading speeds, simple website navigation, and a user-friendly experience across all platforms (desktop and mobile) should all be part of mobile optimization. Businesses will have a better chance of remaining competitive in the shifting landscape if they take these easy actions now!

Challenges in Digital Marketing

Data Privacy and Regulations

Data privacy has become a paramount concern and challenge for digital marketers in recent years. The increasing focus on data protection and privacy regulations and rising consumer awareness about their rights have reshaped how businesses collect, use, and handle personal information. This challenge encompasses a range of complexities that require meticulous attention and compliance.

Significance of Data Privacy

Data privacy is safeguarding individuals' personal information, ensuring it is collected and used responsibly and with the consent of the data subjects. In the digital marketing context, personal data often includes names, email addresses, phone numbers, browsing habits, and even more sensitive information like financial details or health records. The significance of data privacy in digital marketing can be summarized as follows:

- **Consumer Trust:** Respecting data privacy builds trust with customers. When individuals trust that their data is handled carefully, they are more likely to engage with brands and share information willingly.

- **Compliance and Legal Obligations:** Numerous regulations, such as the General Data Protection Regulation (GDPR) in the European Union, the California Consumer Privacy Act (CCPA), and more, mandate how businesses must handle personal data. Non-compliance can lead to substantial fines and legal consequences.

- **Reputation Management:** Mishandling of data can result in negative publicity and damage a brand's reputation. In an age of social media and online reviews, reputation management is critical.

- **Data Security:** Protecting customer data is a legal requirement and a moral and ethical responsibility. Data breaches can have severe consequences, including financial losses and damage to customer relationships.

Challenges of Data Privacy and Regulations

- **Complexity of Regulations:** Data privacy regulations are often complex and multifaceted, making it challenging for businesses to interpret and comply with them. The nuances of GDPR, CCPA, and other regional laws require dedicated legal and compliance expertise.

- **Consent Management:** Obtaining explicit consent from individuals for data processing is essential. Managing and documenting this consent across various touchpoints can be cumbersome.

- **Data Governance:** Establishing robust data governance practices, including data mapping, storage, access controls, and encryption, is crucial for compliance but can be resource-intensive.

- **Global Operations:** International businesses must navigate a patchwork of regulations that may conflict or overlap, requiring comprehensive compliance strategies.

- **Third-Party Data:** Managing data from third-party sources presents risks, as businesses are responsible for ensuring the data's legality and consent.

- **Data Security:** Ensuring data security is a continuous challenge. Cybersecurity threats and data breaches are real dangers that can result in substantial legal and financial liabilities.

Navigating Data Privacy Challenges

Navigating the challenges of data privacy and regulations in digital marketing requires a proactive and comprehensive approach:

- **Education and Training:** Invest in educating your team on data privacy regulations, their implications, and best practices for compliance. Regular training updates are essential.

- **Compliance Audits:** Conduct regular compliance audits to assess your data practices and identify areas of improvement. Seek legal counsel if necessary.

- **Transparency:** Be transparent with your customers about collecting, using, and protecting their data. Develop clear and accessible privacy policies.

- **Consent Management Platforms:** Implement consent management platforms to streamline the process of obtaining, managing, and documenting user consent.

- **Data Minimization:** Collect only the data necessary for your marketing efforts, reducing the potential risks of handling excessive information.

- **Secure Data Handling:** Prioritize data security with encryption, secure storage, and access controls. Prepare an incident response plan in case of data breaches.

- **Privacy by Design:** Incorporate privacy considerations into the design of your products, services, and marketing campaigns from the outset.

- **Global Compliance:** If your operations span multiple regions, adopt a global compliance strategy considering the most stringent regulations.

Ad Blocking

Ad blocking is a significant challenge that digital marketers and advertisers have had to grapple with in recent years. It refers to using software or browser extensions to prevent ads from displaying on websites and mobile apps. This phenomenon has gained popularity among internet users for several reasons and has significant implications for the digital marketing industry. Let's explore ad blocking in greater detail:

Reasons for the Rise of Ad Blocking

- **User Experience:** Advertisements, especially intrusive ones like pop-ups, auto-playing videos, and large banners, can disrupt the user experience and make websites less enjoyable to visit.

- **Privacy Concerns:** Users are increasingly concerned about their online privacy. Advertisements often rely on tracking user behavior to deliver targeted ads, which some find invasive.

- **Page Load Speed:** Ads can significantly slow down webpage loading times, leading users to seek ways to improve their browsing experience.

- **Security:** Malvertising, where malicious software is delivered through ads, is a growing concern. Ad blockers can provide an additional layer of security against such threats.

Implications and Challenges for Digital Marketers

- **Reduced Reach:** Ad blocking diminishes the reach of digital advertising. It limits the number of users who see ads, potentially affecting campaign performance.

- **Monetization Challenges:** Publishers, especially those dependent on ad revenue, may struggle to generate income if a significant portion of their audience blocks ads. This could lead to the adoption of alternative revenue models or subscription-based content.

- **Ad Quality:** To bypass ad blockers, some advertisers resort to more intrusive or deceptive advertising practices, which can worsen the user experience and lead to a negative perception of brands.

- **Analytics and Data Accuracy:** Ad blockers can interfere with tracking and analytics tools, making it challenging to accurately measure campaign performance and user behavior.

Strategies to Navigate the Ad Blocking Challenge

- **Acceptable Ads:** Some ad blockers allow "acceptable ads" to pass through, provided they meet certain criteria like non-intrusiveness. Marketers can design ads that adhere to these standards.

- **Native Advertising:** Native ads blend seamlessly with the content of a webpage, making them less likely to be blocked. They are often perceived as less intrusive and more engaging.

- **Content Marketing:** Invest in content marketing strategies that provide valuable, non-promotional content. Content marketing can engage users without relying heavily on traditional display advertising.

- **Improved User Experience:** Prioritize user experience by reducing ad clutter, improving site speed, and avoiding disruptive ad formats.

- **Diversified Channels:** Explore advertising on platforms where ad blocking is less prevalent, such as social media and mobile apps, to diversify your marketing efforts.

- **Transparency and Privacy:** Address user concerns about privacy by being transparent about data collection and use. Implement data protection measures and comply with privacy regulations like GDPR.

- **Innovation:** Invest in innovative ad formats, such as interactive and immersive ads, that provide value to users rather than interrupting their experience.

Content Saturation

Content saturation is a significant challenge in the digital marketing landscape. It refers to the overwhelming abundance of online content, making it increasingly difficult for marketers to capture the attention of their target audience and stand out in a crowded digital space. This phenomenon has several implications for digital marketers, and understanding its nuances is essential for crafting effective strategies. Below, we elaborate on the concept of content saturation and the challenges it poses:

Overwhelming Volume of Content: The internet is flooded with content. Millions of blog posts, articles, videos, social media updates, and other forms of content are published daily. This sheer volume of information creates a competitive environment where brands and marketers must vie for their audience's limited attention.

Decreased Visibility: Content saturation leads to decreased visibility for individual pieces of content. When numerous brands are publishing content on the same topics or using the same keywords, it becomes challenging for any single piece of content to rank well in search engines or gain prominence on social media.

Audience Overwhelm: Consumers are bombarded with content from all directions. As a result, they may experience information overload, causing them to disengage or tune out content that doesn't immediately resonate with their needs or interests.

Quality vs. Quantity: The emphasis has shifted from quantity to quality. While publishing a high volume of content was once seen as a strategy for visibility, now, quality trumps quantity. Brands must invest more time and resources in creating valuable, relevant, and engaging content to capture and maintain their audience's attention.

Difficulty in Originality: Originality is increasingly difficult to achieve in a saturated content landscape. It's challenging to develop unique angles or perspectives on topics that have been extensively covered. This poses a creative challenge for content creators.

Shortened Attention Spans: Consumers' attention spans have shortened in response to the constant barrage of information. Marketers must create content quickly, grabbing and retaining the audience's attention. This often means concise, visually appealing, and immediately engaging content.

Content Promotion Costs: With the rise of content saturation, marketers may need to allocate more budget for content promotion. It's no longer sufficient to rely solely on organic reach; paid advertising or sponsored content may be necessary to ensure visibility.

Diminished SEO Impact: Search engine optimization (SEO) is affected by content saturation. Ranking becomes more challenging with so much content competing for top positions in search results. Marketers must employ advanced SEO techniques and focus on niche or long-tail keywords to improve visibility.

Strategies for Navigating Content Saturation

- **In-Depth, Niche Content:** Focus on creating content that delves deeply into specific niche topics. High-quality, specialized content can stand out in a sea of generic material.

- **Content Distribution:** Diversify your content distribution channels. Besides your website and social media, consider platforms like podcasts, webinars, or niche forums where your audience might be more engaged.

- **Audience-Centric Approach:** Understand your audience's pain points, interests, and preferences. Tailor your content to meet their specific needs, increasing the chances of engagement.

- **Repurposing and Updating:** Repurpose and update existing content. This allows you to breathe new life into older material and keep it relevant.

- **Effective Promotion:** Invest in content promotion and distribution strategies. Use paid advertising, influencer partnerships, and email marketing to amplify your reach.

- **Measurement and Optimization:** Continuously measure the performance of your content. Use analytics to refine your content strategy, focusing on what resonates best with your audience.

Algorithm Changes

In digital marketing, algorithm changes pose a significant and ongoing challenge for professionals and businesses alike. Algorithms employed by search engines and social media platforms determine the visibility and ranking of content. These algorithms are dynamic, frequently evolving, and can profoundly impact digital marketing strategies. In this explanation, we will delve into why algorithm changes are a challenge and explore strategies for effectively navigating this ever-shifting landscape.

The Inherent Complexity of Algorithms: One of the core challenges stems from the complexity of algorithms. Companies like Google, Facebook, and Instagram employ intricate algorithms considering numerous factors when ranking content. These factors include user behavior, content quality, relevance, and engagement metrics. The complexity of these algorithms makes it challenging for marketers to predict how changes will impact their content's visibility.

Frequent Updates and Changes: Digital platforms continuously refine and update their algorithms to improve user experiences and combat spammy or low-quality content. These frequent updates mean that what worked well in a digital marketing strategy one month may no longer be effective the next. This necessitates ongoing vigilance and adaptation by marketers.

Impact on Organic Reach: Algorithm changes often result in shifts in organic reach. Marketers who have invested time and effort into optimizing their content for previous algorithms may find their organic reach suddenly diminished. This can be frustrating, particularly for smaller businesses with limited resources to adapt quickly.

Paid Advertising Costs: Algorithm changes can also affect paid advertising costs. A significant algorithm alteration can lead to fluctuations in advertising costs and conversion rates, impacting the ROI of digital advertising campaigns.

Balancing User Experience: Digital platforms aim to prioritize user experience and satisfaction. Algorithm changes are often driven by a desire to surface the most relevant and engaging content for users. Marketers must navigate the challenge of creating content that aligns with platform algorithms while still delivering value to their audience.

Navigating Algorithm Changes

Despite the challenges posed by algorithm changes, there are strategies that digital marketers can employ to adapt effectively:

- **Stay Informed:** Regularly monitor industry news and updates from digital platforms to stay informed about algorithm changes.

- **Diversify Platforms:** Relying solely on one platform is risky. Diversify your digital marketing efforts across multiple platforms to mitigate the impact of algorithm changes on any single channel.

- **Quality Content:** Focus on creating high-quality, valuable, and relevant content. Algorithms often prioritize content that resonates with users.

- **Analytics and Testing:** Utilize analytics tools to measure the performance of your content and campaigns. A/B testing can help identify the best strategies in the current algorithmic landscape.

- **Adapt Quickly:** Be agile in adjusting your strategies in response to algorithm changes. Waiting too long to adapt can result in missed opportunities and decreased visibility.

- **Ethical Practices:** Avoid tactics that violate platform guidelines, such as keyword stuffing or clickbait. Ethical practices build long-term trust with platforms and audiences.

Trends in Digital Marketing

Digital marketing is a dynamic field that continually evolves in response to technological advancements, consumer behavior changes, and industry priority shifts. Staying informed about the latest trends is crucial for marketers to adapt, remain competitive, and achieve their marketing objectives. In this essay, we'll explore some of the prominent trends in digital marketing as of my last knowledge update in September 2021.

Video Marketing Dominance

- **Live Streaming:** Live video content on platforms like Facebook Live, Instagram Live, and YouTube Live gained traction. It offers real-time engagement and authentic interactions with audiences.

- **Short-Form Videos:** The popularity of short-form video content on platforms like TikTok and Instagram Reels led to increased brand adoption.

Content Personalization

- **Hyper-Personalization:** Marketers used data-driven insights to create highly personalized content, offers, and recommendations for individual users.

- **Behavioral Trigger Campaigns:** Automated campaigns triggered by user behavior, such as abandoned cart emails or personalized product recommendations, became more prevalent.

Voice Search Optimization

- **Voice Assistants:** With the growing use of voice-activated devices like Amazon Echo and Google Home, optimizing content for voice search became a priority.

- **Long-Tail Keywords:** Marketers focused on long-tail keywords and natural language queries to align with how people speak to voice assistants.

Artificial Intelligence (AI) and Machine Learning

- **Predictive Analytics:** AI-driven predictive analytics helped marketers anticipate customer behavior and tailor content and recommendations accordingly.

- **Chatbots and Virtual Assistants:** Chatbots equipped with AI capabilities improved customer service, handling inquiries, and providing personalized responses.

Ephemeral Content

- **Stories Format:** The Stories format on platforms like Instagram, Facebook, and Snapchat gained momentum. Marketers leveraged it for real-time engagement and promotions.

- **Disappearing Content:** Disappearing content creates a sense of urgency and was used for limited-time offers and exclusive promotions.

Social Commerce

- **In-App Shopping:** Social media platforms integrated shopping features, allowing users to discover and purchase products without leaving the app.

- **Shoppable Posts:** Brands used shoppable posts on platforms like Instagram to facilitate direct product purchases.

Privacy and Data Protection

- **Data Privacy Regulations:** Compliance with data privacy regulations, like GDPR and CCPA, became a priority. Marketers had to be transparent about data usage and obtain user consent.

- **First-Party Data:** Marketers focused on collecting and leveraging first-party data to reduce reliance on third-party cookies and improve personalization.

User-Generated Content (UGC)

- **UGC Campaigns:** Brands encouraged customers to create and share content related to their products or services. UGC added authenticity to marketing efforts.

- **Social Proof:** UGC served as social proof, influencing potential customers' decisions.

Interactive Content

- **Polls, Quizzes, and Surveys:** Interactive content like polls and quizzes engaged audiences and provided valuable insights into consumer preferences.

- **Augmented Reality (AR):** AR experiences, such as virtual try-ons for cosmetics or furniture, enhanced customer engagement.

Sustainability and Social Responsibility

- **Cause Marketing:** Brands incorporated sustainability and social responsibility into their messaging and practices, aligning with consumer values.

- **Eco-Friendly Initiatives:** Companies showcased their eco-friendly initiatives and sustainable products.

Mobile-First Approach

- **Mobile Optimization:** As mobile device usage increased, marketers focused on mobile-friendly website design, responsive emails, and mobile advertising.

- **Mobile Advertising:** Mobile advertising, particularly on social media platforms, became a primary channel for reaching consumers.

Navigating Challenges and Trends

- **Continuous Learning**: Staying informed about the latest trends and regulations is paramount. Professionals should invest in ongoing education and training to remain competitive and compliant.

- **Data-Driven Decision-Making**: Marketers should leverage data analytics to make informed decisions. Data can provide insights into consumer behavior, campaign performance, and areas for improvement.

- **Adaptability**: Being adaptable is crucial in the face of rapid changes. Marketers must be open to experimentation and quick to adjust their strategies based on the evolving digital landscape.

- **Content Quality**: In the age of content saturation, the quality of content trumps quantity. Brands should prioritize creating content that genuinely addresses the needs and interests of their audience.

- **Ethical Practices**: Adhering to ethical marketing practices, such as transparency in data collection and responsible advertising, not only ensures compliance but also builds trust with consumers.

- **Collaboration**: Collaborating with peers, influencers, and industry experts can amplify the reach and impact of marketing efforts. Building strategic partnerships can be valuable in navigating challenges and capitalizing on trends.

FUTURE OF DIGITAL MARKETING CONTENT

I n the future of digital marketing, evolving tools, trends, and technology pave the way for capitalizing on new opportunities. On the other hand, keeping up with frequent improvements can be a daunting chore for site owners. Here are the future predictions for the major digital marketing trends:

- In 2023, 50% of marketers want to boost their content marketing expenses, with 1 in 5 increasing by double digits.

- Social media presently accounts for 33% of all digital ad spending and is expected to grow further in the future.

- 45% of small businesses already have a sponsored search strategy in place, and that percentage will grow as the need for high-quality content grows.

- 61% of customers like to shop and are likelier to buy from firms offering augmented reality services.

- Take advantage of improving technology and expand your business with the top digital marketing trends.

Everyone will be talking about three significant future digital marketing developments. The first is the revival of Content Marketing as the primary marketing strategy for organizations. Before the pandemic, startup founders and B2B SaaS marketers might contemplate purchasing social media ads to help their businesses grow. They are now focusing even more on content marketing.

Why? Because Google stated that content marketing is the most effective approach to rank for buyer searches. According to the Content Marketing Institute, 50% of businesses will boost their content marketing expenses in 2023, with one-fifth increasing by double digits.

The second major trend is artificial intelligence-generated content. We will begin to see the value of an AI-powered content marketing strategy. If we waste 60-70% of our stuff, AI will begin to compel us to reexamine what we create and why. For over two years, publications like the Washington Post and others have used AI to generate templated content.

Employee activation is the third most important trend. While AI will tell us what to develop, our best storytellers are our current people from across the organization. Every organization requires a strategy to engage these people as both content creators and the most effective distribution route for that material. This is what we call The AI Paradox: the more machines advise humans what to do, the more marketing people we'll need to generate and distribute that content.

Other Future Digital Marketing Trends

Voice-powered Everything

Smart speakers and "assistants" have been around for a while, but they truly took off in 2017 and 2018 as people lost their fear of talking to their phones and a slew of new consumer gadgets, such as Amazon Alexa and Google Home, hit the market.

There's no reason to expect this mobile trend to slow off, and this hands-free technology will become an increasingly common way for consumers to engage with their gadgets. It is estimated that voice search powers more than half of all search inquiries.

With the increase of voice search-enabled smart gadgets, there will be additional options to promote to those who own them. Amazon saw this possibility early on when it began providing cheaper Kindle devices in exchange for consenting to receive marketing emails. Targeted Alexa ads are already in the works; additional gadgets will undoubtedly follow.

AI-Powered Marketing and Support Technology

For quite some time, artificial intelligence has been expanding what is feasible in the future of digital marketing, but in the coming years, we will see exponential jumps in what this technology is capable of.

Chatbots will become a customer care standard and will increasingly replace live operators as machine learning algorithms get more powerful and can mimic humans with almost eerie accuracy. Marketing is becoming more conversational and individualized, and chatbots allow you to capitalize on this trend without wasting your staff or resources.

Artificial intelligence is also being employed in advertising. While it hasn't yet attained human-level creativity, Google is already using AI-powered ads to optimize campaigns by finding the best-performing ad designs and language and automatically updating based on user engagement.

The Social Media Future

You may believe that social media is already ubiquitous, yet it still has the opportunity to expand. Social media presently accounts for 33% of all digital ad spending and is expected to grow further. While the future of social media may be something, well, more social, the expansion of these platforms is unlikely to slow anytime soon.

Social media will continue to infiltrate every aspect of our lives and become genuinely integrated with both online and offline services. In an episode of the dystopian Netflix series Black Mirror, social networking has overflowed into the real world, with people rating their interactions with others and being rewarded better housing, jobs, and social standing based on their total rating.

Is it science fiction? Maybe for now, but the future isn't so far away. Most of your phone's apps are probably already exchanging data with your social media networks, and companies and recruiters are increasingly screening social media accounts before interviews.

So, what does this imply for marketers? As AI algorithms employed in social media get more advanced, there will be a better understanding of each client as an individual and the ability to give more targeted offers and services.

The Rise of Micro-influencer Marketing

Influencer marketing has already increased in popularity in recent years, with top influencers on platforms such as Instagram and YouTube acquiring millions of followers and earning six figures from brand partnerships.

However, influencer marketing is still in its infancy, and while it promises a higher ROI than more traditional advertising channels, there are still kinks to work out. Fake followers are a contemporary issue that is still being addressed, and there have been some prominent instances when brand/influencer connections have backfired negatively.

Big-name influencers are also losing power as they accept more and more sponsored postings, which reduces the validity and impact of their recommendations. As consumers continue to value personal recommendations over being marketed to, spending more on "micro-influencers" - those social media users with a tiny but loyal following who can offer truly authentic marketing messages to a trusting audience makes sense.

Influencers' power will be judged not by the amount of followers they have but by their personal interactions with each one.

Augmented Reality Is Becoming More Common

Remember the 2016 Pokémon Go craze? The smartphone game was not only a brilliant illustration of how augmented reality can be applied in video games but also a marketing opportunity, as businesses leaped on the opportunity to sell to clients hoping to catch a Pokémon or two on their doorstep.

Augmented reality is more than just a novelty for gamers. Brands are increasingly using it to reach out to customers. In fact, 61% of customers prefer to buy from firms that offer augmented reality services and are more likely to acquire things from them.

Ikea now has a virtual reality catalog where you can virtually place furniture in your own house, and fashion brands are beginning to use augmented reality to allow clients to virtually try on items in the comfort of their own homes.

Expect more firms to join the augmented reality bandwagon for the technology to become more common with legitimate marketing goals rather than a charming trick.

Video Overtaking All Other Digital Channels

For years, savvy marketers have recognized the importance of online video; The Washington Post forecasted in 2015 that video would account for 80% of all online content by 2020. We're not quite there yet, but the video is already proving to be a powerful medium, with live-streaming video, particularly, seeing a significant increase in the last year or two.

Video marketing can be extremely effective at increasing engagement levels, and the consumer thirst for video shows no signs of abating - YouTube has already surpassed Facebook as the second-most visited site (Google, of course, is number one).

If you haven't properly embraced video in your brand promotion, you're already behind, but it's not too late to catch up. Exciting things are becoming possible with the combination of live video and augmented reality, and original and creative videos will surely be the main content channel winner as we head into next year.

Employee Activation: Getting Back to Basics

Of course, technological advancements are wonderful, but we must not lose sight of the fundamental concepts that define a great marketing plan and a great company.

Employee activation will allow your firm to get the most out of every employee, who will act as a brand ambassador and drive sales and conversions more genuinely and authentically than any advertising campaign could ever be.

It is arguably the most influential B2B marketing trend right now!

Referencing the micro-influencer marketing trend, when your staff are engaged, they will function as micro-influencers for your brand. If you are successful in hiring employees who share your brand values and share their enthusiasm for what you are attempting to grow, they will serve as your most ardent supporters.

As our reliance on technology grows, more and more organizations recognize the need to be more "human" and activate employees' storytelling and organic sharing power - this is the "paradox of AI" as we learn to coexist with machines in this brave new world of opportunities.

Outsourcing to Digital Marketing Agencies

Outsourcing to a digital marketing agency can help you develop more content, whether a small or large business. Creating enough high-quality content with in-house resources is difficult and can prevent you from capitalizing on growth prospects.

Digital marketing is critical to success because it is the greatest way to rank on Google. So why not enlist the assistance of marketing experts? In 2023, 45% of small firms will have a sponsored search strategy in place, which is anticipated to climb. The assistance of trained specialists is frequently the difference between making little progress and witnessing big, ongoing developments in traffic and sales. By outsourcing to digital marketing services, you can sit back, relax, and watch your business develop this year.

Staying Inspired: Resources, Communities, and Learning from Industry Leaders

Staying inspired and continuously evolving is not a luxury but a necessity. The digital landscape evolves rapidly, and marketing strategies that were effective yesterday may become obsolete tomorrow. To thrive in this environment, marketers must seek inspiration from diverse sources, engage in communities, and learn from industry leaders. Let's see how these practices can contribute to professional growth and success.

Resources for Continuous Learning

The foundation of staying inspired in digital marketing is a commitment to lifelong learning. The field is marked by constant innovation and change, making it imperative for marketers to keep their knowledge up-to-date. Fortunately, numerous resources are available for this purpose.

Firstly, the digital marketing space is replete with online courses and certifications. Platforms like Coursera, LinkedIn Learning, and HubSpot Academy offer courses on various digital marketing aspects, from SEO to social media marketing. These structured courses provide a systematic way to acquire new skills and knowledge.

Additionally, blogs and industry publications serve as valuable resources. Following authoritative blogs like Moz, Neil Patel, and Search Engine Journal allows marketers to access the latest trends, strategies, and case studies. Subscribing to industry newsletters ensures that professionals are informed about critical updates and developments.

Moreover, podcasts and webinars have become prominent sources of insights and inspiration. Podcasts like "Marketing Over Coffee" and "The Smart Passive Income Podcast" offer in-depth discussions on digital marketing trends and strategies. Webinars hosted by industry experts provide a platform for interactive learning and exchanging ideas.

Engaging in Communities

Communities are pivotal in staying inspired and connected in the digital marketing realm. Joining industry-specific forums, groups, and social media communities can provide a sense of belonging and foster creativity.

LinkedIn Groups, Reddit communities like r/marketing, and industry-specific forums like Moz's Whiteboard Friday are excellent networking and knowledge-sharing platforms. These communities provide opportunities to seek advice, discuss challenges, and learn from peers' experiences.

Participating in industry-related events and conferences also enables marketers to connect with like-minded professionals. Events like Content Marketing World and Social Media Marketing World offer networking opportunities and exposure to the latest trends and technologies.

Learning from Industry Leaders

Learning from industry leaders is a cornerstone of staying inspired and achieving professional growth in digital marketing. These leaders serve as beacons of innovation and expertise, offering valuable insights through their experiences and thought leadership.

One effective way to learn from industry leaders is through mentorship or coaching relationships. Establishing a mentorship with a seasoned professional can provide guidance, constructive feedback, and a broader perspective on industry dynamics.

Additionally, following thought leaders and experts on social media platforms and subscribing to their newsletters can provide a steady stream of insights and inspiration. Engaging with their content, asking questions, and participating in discussions can lead to valuable interactions and learning experiences.

Attending keynote sessions, webinars, or panel discussions featuring industry leaders at conferences and events provides direct access to their expertise. These events often showcase the latest trends and best practices, allowing attendees to absorb knowledge and strategies directly from the experts.

All in all, this proactive approach benefits individual marketers and contributes to the advancement of the digital marketing industry as a whole.

CONCLUSION

In the fast-paced and ever-evolving realm of digital marketing, success is often synonymous with adaptability and innovation. To thrive in this dynamic landscape, you must cultivate a mindset of continuous improvement and creativity. This mindset fuels personal and professional growth and enables marketers to stay at the forefront of their field. Let's explore the significance of embracing such a mindset and provide actionable insights for nurturing it.

Embracing Continuous Improvement

Continuous improvement is a philosophy that encourages individuals and organizations to constantly seek ways to enhance their processes, skills, and knowledge. This mindset is indispensable in digital marketing, where strategies and technologies evolve rapidly.

Lifelong Learning: The cornerstone of continuous improvement is lifelong learning. Digital marketers must stay updated with their field's latest trends, tools, and strategies. This involves regular participation in webinars, conferences, workshops, and online courses.

Data-Driven Decision-Making: Data is the lifeblood of digital marketing. Embracing continuous improvement means developing strong analytical skills and using data to inform and refine strategies. Marketers should regularly analyze key performance indicators (KPIs) and use insights to make informed decisions.

A/B Testing and Experimentation: A culture of experimentation is vital for growth. Marketers should frequently conduct A/B tests to refine their strategies. Experimentation allows for discovering what works best for a specific audience or campaign.

Fostering Creativity

Creativity is the catalyst that propels digital marketing campaigns from ordinary to extraordinary. It involves thinking outside the box, finding novel solutions, and creating content that resonates deeply with the audience.

- **Cross-Disciplinary Knowledge:** Creativity often thrives at the intersection of different fields. Marketers should seek inspiration from diverse sources such as psychology, design, technology, and even art. Cross-disciplinary knowledge can lead to fresh ideas and innovative approaches.

- **Collaborative Environments:** Encouraging collaboration within a team can spark creativity. Brainstorming sessions, idea sharing, and diverse perspectives can lead to breakthroughs. Encourage team members to share their unique insights and experiences.

- **Embracing Failure:** Creativity often involves taking risks, and the possibility of failure comes with risk. A mindset of continuous improvement and creativity means embracing failure as a valuable learning experience. Failures provide insights that can lead to future successes.

Actionable Insights for Nurturing this Mindset:

To actively embrace a mindset of continuous improvement and creativity, consider the following steps:

- **Set Clear Goals:** Define your personal and professional goals. These goals will serve as your compass, guiding your efforts toward improvement and creativity.

- **Create a Learning Plan:** Identify areas where you want to improve and create a structured learning plan. Allocate time for reading, courses, and skill development.

- **Keep a Journal:** Maintain a journal to record insights, ideas, and lessons learned. Review it regularly to track your progress and maintain a sense of continuity in your improvement journey.

- **Seek Feedback:** Solicit feedback from peers, mentors, or colleagues. Constructive criticism can provide valuable insights for improvement.

- **Cultivate Creativity Rituals:** Develop routines or rituals that stimulate creativity. This could involve activities like meditation, brainstorming sessions, or simply setting aside time for unstructured thinking.

- **Celebrate Small Wins:** Recognize and celebrate even minor accomplishments. This positive reinforcement can fuel motivation and creativity.

Those who foster creativity through cross-disciplinary knowledge, collaboration, and resilience in the face of failure will have the edge in crafting innovative and compelling marketing campaigns. This combination of continuous improvement and creativity enables digital marketers to thrive and lead in their field.

So far, we have seen that "Digital Marketing Content Creation: Engaging Your Target Audience" is a comprehensive guide that equips digital marketers with the knowledge and strategies needed to excel in the ever-evolving digital marketing landscape. Throughout this book, we've explored the intricate world of content creation and distribution, emphasizing the crucial role of content in building relationships, driving conversions, and establishing brand authority.

In the initial chapters, we delved into the foundational aspects of digital marketing content creation, including understanding your audience, setting content goals, and crafting compelling content. We also uncovered the secrets of optimizing content for search engines, social media platforms, and email marketing.

As we progressed, we dissected the intricacies of creating content tailored for various social media platforms, delving into strategies for crafting shareable and viral content. We also discussed the importance of engaging with your audience, building a sense of community, and leveraging trends and memes.

Video and visual content creation, as highlighted in Chapter 6, was unveiled as a powerful tool in the digital marketing arsenal, with insights on planning, shooting, and editing captivating videos and creating visually appealing content.

Furthermore, personalization and segmentation were unveiled as strategies to enhance relevance and engagement, and we explored automation and dynamic content as practical tools for efficient personalization.

Chapter 8 guided us through content distribution and promotion, detailing multichannel distribution strategies, paid promotion, and methods to maximize organic reach through social sharing, SEO, and email marketing.

In Chapters 9 and 10, we emphasized the significance of building relationships and authority through thought leadership, content collaborations, and backlink strategies. We also addressed challenges such as content overload and the importance of ethical content practices.

Lastly, the final chapter explored the future of digital marketing content, offering insights into emerging trends such as AI-generated content, voice search, and interactive experiences. We emphasized the importance of continuous learning and staying inspired through resources, communities, and learning from industry leaders.

In this ever-evolving digital marketing landscape, the journey to success requires dedication, adaptability, and a commitment to staying informed and inspired. "Digital Marketing Content Creation: Engaging Your Target Audience" serves as a roadmap for both seasoned professionals and newcomers, helping them navigate the complexities of digital marketing content with confidence and creativity. As the digital marketing landscape continues to evolve, this book empowers marketers to keep pace and lead the way in this dynamic and exciting field.

www.ingramcontent.com/pod-product-compliance
Lightning Source LLC
Chambersburg PA
CBHW071645210326
41597CB00017B/2118